THINKING
AS A SCIENCE

BY

HENRY HAZLITT

NEW YORK

E. P. DUTTON & COMPANY

681 FIFTH AVENUE

Copyright, 1916
By E. P. DUTTON & COMPANY

CONTENTS

THINKING AS A SCIENCE

I

THE NEGLECT OF THINKING

EVERY man knows there are evils in the world which need setting right. Every man has pretty definite ideas as to what these evils are. But to most men one in particular stands out vividly. To some, in fact, this stands out with such startling vividness that they lose sight of other evils, or look upon them as the natural consequences of their own particular evil-in-chief.

To the Socialist this evil is the capitalistic system; to the prohibitionist it is intemperance; to the feminist it is the subjection of women; to the clergyman it is the decline of religion; to Andrew Carnegie it is war; to the staunch Republican it is the Democratic Party, and so on, *ad infinitum.*

1

I, too, have a pet little evil, to which in more passionate moments I am apt to attribute all the others. This evil is the neglect of thinking. And when I say thinking I mean real thinking, independent thinking, hard thinking.

You protest. You say men are thinking more now than they ever were. You bring out the almanac to prove by statistics that illiteracy is declining. You point to our magnificent libraries. You point to the multiplication of books. You show beyond a doubt that people are reading more now than ever before in all history. . . .

Very well, exactly. That is just the trouble. Most people, when confronted with a problem, immediately acquire an inordinate desire to "read-up" on it. When they get stuck mentally, the first thing such people do is to run to a book. Confess it, have you not often been in a waiting room or a Pullman, noticed people all about you reading, and finding yourself without any reading matter, have you not wished that you had some?—something to "occupy your mind"? And did it ever occur to you that you had within you the power to occupy

your mind, and do it more profitably than all
those assiduous readers? Briefly, did it ever
occur to you to *think?*

Of course you "thought"—in a sense.
Thinking means a variety of things. You may
have looked out of your train window while
passing a field, and it may have occurred to you
that that field would make an excellent baseball
diamond. Then you "thought" of the time
when you played baseball, "thought" of some
particular game perhaps, "thought" how you
had made a grand stand play or a bad muff,
and how one day it began to rain in the middle
of the game, and the team took refuge in the
carriage shed. Then you "thought" of other
rainy days rendered particularly vivid for
some reason or other, or perhaps your mind
came back to considering the present weather,
and how long it was going to last. . . . And of
course, in one sense you were "thinking." But
when I use the word thinking, I mean thinking
with a purpose, with an end in view, thinking
to solve a problem. I mean the kind of thinking that is forced on us when we are deciding on a course to pursue, on a life work to

take up perhaps; the kind of thinking that was forced on us in our younger days when we had to find a solution to a problem in mathematics, or when we tackled psychology in college. I do not mean "thinking" in snatches, or holding petty opinions on this subject and on that. I mean thought on significant questions which lie outside the bounds of your narrow personal welfare. This is the kind of thinking which is now so rare—so sadly needed!

Of course before this can be revived we must arouse a desire for it. We must arouse a desire for thinking for its own sake; solving problems for the mere sake of solving problems. But a mere desire for thinking, praiseworthy as it is, is not enough. We must know *how* to think, and to that end we must search for those rules and methods of procedure which will most help us in thinking creatively, originally, and not least of all surely, correctly.

When they think at all, the last thing men think about is their own thoughts. Every sensible man realizes that the perfection of a mechanical instrument depends to some extent upon the perfection of the tools with which it is made. No carpenter would expect a perfectly smooth board after using a dented or chipped plane. No gasolene engine manufacturer would expect to produce a good motor unless he had the best lathes obtainable to help him turn out his product. No watchmaker would expect to construct a perfectly accurate timepiece unless he had the most delicate and accurate tools to turn out the cogs and screws. Before any specialist produces an instrument he thinks of the tools with which he is to produce it. But men reflect continually on the most complex problems—problems of vital importance to them—and expect to obtain satisfactory solutions, without once giving a thought to the manner in which they go about obtaining those solutions; without a thought to their own mind, the tool which produces those solutions. Surely this deserves at least some systematic consideration.

Some remarks of Ella Wheeler Wilcox under this head will bear quoting: "Human thinking is still in as great a state of disorder and jumble as language was before the alphabet, music before the scale was discovered, printing before Gutenberg, or mathematics before Pythagoras formulated its laws.'' ''This systematization of all thought,'' she tells us, would be ''a more far reaching improvement than all the others, for it will do for education, health, economics, government, etc., what the alphabet did for language, movable type for printing and literature, the scale for music, and the rules of arithmetic for calculation. Being the exact counterpart of these in its particular field, its mission, like theirs, will be to bring order out of chaos.''

I believe Miss Wilcox exaggerates matters. Incidentally I for one do not pretend to have discovered anything revolutionary. But the importance of the subject warrants its formulation into as near scientific form as we can bring it.

I beg no one to get frightened. Science does not necessarily mean test tubes and telescopes. I mean science in its broadest sense; and in this sense it means nothing more than organized knowledge. If we are to find rules and methods of procedure, these methods must come from somewhere—must be based on certain principles—and these principles can come only from close, systematic investigation.

It may indeed be urged that we can think best by disregarding all "rules," by not paying any attention to method. But the man who maintains this must give reasons; and once he attempts this he himself is bordering closely on the science of the matter. In short, the settlement of even this question is part of the science of thinking.

And what is to be the nature of this science?

For our purposes, all sciences may be divided into two kinds: *positive* and *normative*. A positive science investigates the nature of things as they are. It deals simply with matters of fact. Such a science is physics, chemistry, psychology. A normative science is one which studies things as they ought to be. As the name implies, it seeks to establish a *norm* or pattern which ought to be adhered to. It studies means of reaching desired ends. To this class belong such sciences as ethics, education, agriculture.

Now these normative sciences, with the exception of ethics, are nearly always referred to either as "arts" or "applied sciences." To both of these terms I technically but strenuously object. I object to the term "art" to designate any set of organized rules for doing a thing, because "art" also means the actual doing of that thing. And this thing may be done, and often is done, in total ignorance of the rules governing it. A man may possess the art of swimming—he may be able to swim—without any previous instruction, without any knowledge of how he ought to hold his body, arms and legs; just as a dog may do the same thing.

I object also to the term "applied science," because to me this term implies that the science it refers to is based on one positive science only. I can think of no so-called applied science which is so based. Hygiene, not alone dependent on physiology, must derive some of its rules from the chemistry of foods, as well as from the sciences of sanitation and ventilation, themselves normative. Agriculture is based not only on biology and botany, but on chemistry and meteorology.

The science of thinking, then, if such a science there be, is normative. Its purpose is to find those methods which will help us to think constructively and correctly.

One more distinction and our preliminaries are over. There are two other sciences with which the science of thinking is liable to become confused; one positive, the other normative.

The positive science is that branch of psychology which deals with the reasoning process and examines the basis of belief. We shall make frequent use of this science in trying to find rules for thinking, but it will not be the only science we shall use, nor will that science be the subject of this book.

The normative science with which the science of thinking may become confused is logic. Indeed, logic has sometimes been called the science of thinking. Now for our purposes logic is a part of the science of thinking, but it is not the part which we are primarily to consider. Its function is merely negative; it consists in leading us from error. The part of the science of thinking in which we are interested deals with those positive rules which will help to make us creative thinkers. . . .

Our ship is headed for the port Truth. Our mind is the engine, the science of thinking the propeller, and logic the rudder. Without our engine, the mind, the propeller of the science of thinking, which transforms our mental energy most effectively into motion, would be useless. Without the propeller, which gives motion, the rudder of logic would be useless. But all three are needed to reach our goal.

And now I must bespeak a little patience. The next chapter, and the one following it, are going to deal very largely with method and methods. They will touch on classification, and a lot of other things to which the plain man has an aversion; to which, at least, he usually evinces no very active interest. But it is necessary to consider these things in order to make our study complete.

II

THINKING WITH METHOD

MOST of us, at those rare intervals when we think at all, do so in a slipshod sort of way. If we come across a mental difficulty we try to get rid of it in almost any kind of hit or miss manner. Even those few of us who think occasionally for the mere sake of thinking, generally do so without regard for method —indeed, are often unconscious that method could be applied to our thought. But what is meant by method? I may best explain by an example.

From somewhere or other, a man gets hold of the idea that the proper subjects are not being taught in our schools and colleges. He asks himself what the proper subjects would be. He considers how useless his knowledge of Greek and Latin has been. He decides that these two subjects should be eliminated. Then

11

he thinks how he would have been helped in business by a knowledge of bookkeeping, and he concludes that this subject deserves a place in the
curriculum. He has recently received a letter
from a college friend containing some errors in
spelling. He is convinced that this branch of
knowledge is being left in undeserved neglect.
Or he is impressed by the spread of unsound
theories of money among the poorer classes, and
he believes that everybody should receive a
thorough course in economics and finance. And
so he rambles on, now on this subject, now on
that.

Compare this haphazard, aimless thinking
with that of the man of method. This man is
confronted with the same general situation as
our first thinker, but he makes his problem a
different one. He first asks himself what end
he has in view. He discovers that he is primarily trying to find out not so much—what
subjects should be taught in the schools? as—
what knowledge is of most worth? He puts the
problem definitely before himself in this latter
form. He then sees that the problem—what
knowledge is of *most* worth?, implies that what

is desired is not to find what subjects are of worth and what are not, but what is the *relative* value of subjects. His next step, obviously, is to discover a standard by which the relative value of subjects can be determined; and this, let us say, he finds in the help a knowledge of these subjects gives to complete living. Having decided this, he next classifies in the order of their importance the activities which constitute human life, and follows this by classifying subjects as they prepare for these activities.[1]

Needless to say, the results obtained by this thinker will be infinitely more satisfactory than those arrived at by his unsystematic brother. Method, then, is essential. But how are we to apply it in all cases?

Now there are methods without number, and in many cases a problem will require a method all its own; but we here purpose to take up only those most general in application.

Before considering these methods of thinking, however, it would be well to ask ourselves what thinking is. As stated before, the term is

[1] See Herbert Spencer, *Education.*

loosely used to cover a wide range of mental processes. These processes we may roughly divide into memory, imagination and reasoning. It is the last only with which we have to deal. I admit that development of the memory is desirable. I admit that development of the imagination is equally desirable. But they are not the subject of this book. By "thinking" I mean reasoning. And our present purpose is to find the nature of this process.

Modern psychologists tell us that all reasoning begins in perplexity, hesitation, doubt. "The process of reasoning is one of problem solving. . . . The occasion for the reasoning is always a thwarted purpose." [2]

It is essential we keep this in mind. It differs from the popular conception even more than may appear at first sight. *If a man were to know everything he could not think.* Nothing would ever puzzle him, his purposes would never be thwarted, he would never experience perplexity or doubt, he would have no problems. If we are to conceive of God as an All-Knower, we cannot conceive of Him as a Thinking Be-

[2] Pillsbury, *Essentials of Psychology.*

ing. Thinking is reserved for beings of finite intelligence.

Were we to study the origin and evolution of thinking, we would doubtless find that thinking arose in just this way—from thwarted purposes. If our lives and the lives of our animal ancestors had always run smoothly, if our every desire were immediately satisfied, if we never met an obstacle in anything we tried to do, thinking would never have appeared on this planet. But adversity forced us to it.

Tickle a frog's left leg, and his right leg will immediately fly up and scratch it. The action is merely what psychologists would call a "reflex." Absolutely no thinking takes place: the frog would do the same thing if you removed its brain. And if you tickle its right leg its left leg would fly up to scratch. But if you tickled both legs at once they could not both fly up and scratch each other. It would be a physical impossibility. Here, then, is a difficulty. The frog hesitates; thinking steps upon the scene. After mature deliberation the frog solves his problem: he holds his left leg still while he scratches it with his right, then he holds his right leg still and scratches that with his left.

We cannot, then, think on "general principles." To try this is like attempting to chew laughing gas. To think at all requires a purpose, no matter how vague. The best thinking, however, requires a definite purpose, and the more definite this purpose the more definite will be our thinking. Therefore in taking up any special line of thought, we must first find just what our end or purpose is, and thus get clearly in mind what our problems are.

Advising a man to ask himself what his problems are may seem absurd. But it is just this confusion as to what they want to know which has driven men into error time and time again. The history of the never-ending philosophical controversy between "materialism" and "idealism" is largely a history of different ways of stating the issue; the progress made is mainly due to the increasing definiteness with which it has been stated.

One of the most frequent sources of confusion in stating questions is in failure to distinguish between what is and what ought to be.

Considering woman suffrage a man will ask himself "What is woman's sphere?," when he really wants to know not what woman's sphere actually is, but what it ought to be. Our first step, then, is to get our problem or problems clearly in mind, and to state them as definitely as possible. A problem properly stated is a problem partly solved.

What we will do next depends on the nature of the question. In the example "What knowledge is of most worth?" we proceeded to look for a criterion of worthiness. And this was really a re-stating of the question. For instead of asking ourselves "What knowledge is of most worth?," we began asking "What knowledge best prepares for complete living?"

Our next move was to classify. This is essential not only to systematic reasoning but to thinking of any kind. Classification is the process of grouping objects according to common qualities. But as almost all objects differ in some qualities and almost all have some qualities in common, it follows that, contrary to common belief, *there is no one classification absolutely essential to any group of objects.* An infinite number of classifications may be made, because every object has an infinite number of attributes, depending on the aspect we take of it. Nor is any one aspect of a thing "truer" than any other. The aspect we take depends entirely on the purpose we have in mind or the problem we wish to solve. As William James pointed out:

"Now that I am writing it is essential that I conceive my paper as a surface for inscription. If I failed to do that I should have to stop my work. But if I wished to light a fire and no other materials were by, the essential way of conceiving the paper would be as combustible material; and I need then have no thought of any of its other destinations. It is really all that it is: a combustible, a writing surface, a thin thing, a hydrocarbonaceous thing, a thing eight inches one way and ten another, a thing just one furlong east of a certain stone in my neighbor's field, an American thing, etc., etc., *ad infinitum.*" [3]

And if the reader insist that these qualities are merely "accidental," and that what the

[3] *Principles of Psychology,* Vol. II, p. 332.

thing really is, is just *paper* and nothing else, the reply is that the reader is intellectually petrified; that though "paper" may be our commonest title for it and may suggest our usual purpose with it, yet that purpose and this title and the properties which this title suggest have in reality nothing sacramental about them.

So because you have classified something from one aspect do not imagine that you are necessarily precluded from classifying it from any other. A man who is studying the theory of money may divide the medium of exchange into standard money and credit currency. But this need not keep him from viewing it as coins, government notes, and bank currency, nor should it prevent him from classifying it into, say (1) hand-to-hand money, (2) written or printed orders of one party to pay specified sums to another, and (3) book accounts.[4] All these classifications will be true; all may be useful for a full comprehension. Every classification should of course be logical; but it is far more essential that it be utilizable.

And while we are treating of utility, we

[4] See William A. Scott, *Money*.

might note that this *pragmatic* method can be applied with profit to nearly all our positive problems. Before starting to solve a question —while deciding, for instance, on the validity of some nice distinction in logic—we should ask ourselves, "What practical difference will it make if I hold one opinion or the other? How will my belief influence my action?"—(using the word "action" in its broadest sense). This may often lead our line of inquiry into more fruitful channels, keep us from making fine but needless distinctions, help us to word our question more relevantly, and lead us to make distinctions where we really need them.

We are now ready to consider in order a number of constructive methods in thinking.

One method applicable to almost all problems is what we may call either the *deductive* or the *à priori* method. This method reaches a conclusion without observation or experiment. It consists in reasoning from previous experience or from established principles to particular facts. It may, however, be used to confirm observation and experiment as well as to take their place. Take the all important question in biology of whether or not specific characteristics acquired by an animal during its life time are inherited by offspring. The a priori method would examine the structures of the body, the germ plasm from which the offspring develops, and the relation between them, and would ask just how a specific change in the body could affect the germ. If it were found that the tissues that are to continue the race were set off so completely from the structures of the body as to make inconceivable any manner by which they could be influenced by changes in these structures, then this method would decide that acquired characteristics are not transmitted.

Let us take another example. Both the supporters and opponents of woman suffrage have often decided the question without consulting at all the actual results achieved in the States where women vote. They have settled the question to their own satisfaction merely on a priori grounds. They have considered woman's supposed mental qualities as compared with man's, and have decided on her fitness for the ballot solely from these considerations. It must be remembered, however, that before women were admitted to suffrage anywhere, deductive or a priori reasoning was the only kind possible.

It is often helpful to look at a problem from the viewpoint of different sciences. A problem in political science will very likely have an economic aspect, whether it concerns taxation, tariff, trusts or the ownership of land, and so we may look at the question solely from the viewpoint of economics. But the problem may also have an ethical aspect. If it is proposed to pass a universal prohibition law, you may ask, "Has the Government the right to interfere in this way with personal liberty?" Again, we could take a psychological view: we would decide from our knowledge of human nature just what the effect of an alcohol prohibition law would be—whether it would not drive men to even more dangerous drugs, such as morphine and opium.

And now we come to a whole host of effective methods, all of which may be classed as comparative. The comparative method is as old as thought itself, but it is strange that even scientists did not begin to use it consciously and consistently until almost the present generation. Nowhere is it better illustrated than in modern psychology. Most of the so-called branches of psychology are merely different forms of the comparative method of treatment. "Abnormal psychology" is merely a comparison of abnormal mental types with normal mental types for the light they throw on each other. "Child study" is a comparison of the mind of the child with that of the adult. "Animal psychology" is a comparison of the actions of animals with each other and with those of man. And none of these methods is of any value except in so far as it makes use of comparison.

Often consciously used in the consideration of problems is the so-called historical method. This method, as its name implies, consists in obtaining knowledge of a thing by considering its past record. The word history is popularly used in so narrow a sense, however, being restricted only to the history of nations, and often merely to the political history of nations, that we can avoid confusion by calling this method the evolutionary. In the final analysis the method is comparative, for it really consists in comparing a thing at one period of development with itself at another period.

Let us take our example from political science. The historical method, in its popular sense, has been so much used here, even to the exclusion of other methods, that it would seem needless to speak of it. But often the method has been abused and often it has not been given broad enough treatment. It traces the growth of an institution, or of an idea—personal liberty, say,—through successive periods. It notes what the path has been, and judges of the probable future tendency. But a far broader outlook than we get from this narrowly conceived "historical" method is furnished by evolutionary sociology. Here we inquire into the origin of society and of the various trades, industries, professions and pursuits of all kinds, and to do this we go far into prehistoric times.

Nowhere is the evolutionary method more strikingly seen than in biology. Since Darwin's great theory was promulgated the science has gone forward by leaps and bounds. We have derived untold benefit from a comparison of man and animals in the light of this hypothesis; even study of the development of individual man has been aided. The discovery of the *fact* of evolution constituted an incalculable advance, but the method for study which it furnished was of even greater importance.

I have spoken of the comparison of man and animals "in the light of this (evolutionary) hypothesis." This brings us to a point which must be kept in mind in practically all observation. We are often exhorted to "observe." Presumably we are to do this "on general principles." Such advice is about as foolish as asking us to think on general principles. Imagine for the moment what would happen if you started right now to "observe" as much as you could. You might begin with this book and notice the size of the type, the amount of margin, the quality of the paper, the dimensions of the page, the number of pages. But you have by no means exhausted the number of properties possessed by this book. You must observe that it is also combustible, that it is destructible, that it is machine made, that it is American printed, that it is such and such a price, that it weighs so many ounces, that it is flat, that it is rectangular, that its thickness is so much. . . .

The absurdity is obvious. If we started out merely to observe, with no definite purpose in mind, we could keep it up forever. And get nowhere. Nine out of every ten observations would never be put to use. We would be sinfully wasting our time. To observe most profitably, just as to think most profitably, we must have a definite purpose. This purpose must be *to test the truth of a supposition*. A concrete example will make this clear.

A man has been shipwrecked on an island and believes himself to be alone there. One day, as he is walking along the beach, he discovers footprints. How did they get there? His first assumption is that they are his own. It occurs to him, however, that he had not been near this spot for over a week, and that yesterday's storm would have washed any footprints away. This objection is confirmed by making a footprint himself and comparing it with the one observed, and noticing that they differ markedly. The footprints being those of some one else, how did the man who made them get there? The first supposition is that he came in a boat. The idea of a small boat is dismissed because of the assumed great distance of this island from other land. Therefore the man must have come in a large vessel. But the footprints lead to a wet part of the sand and the tide is just going down. In this case they are very recent—made not more than a half hour ago. This being so the man who made them could not have had time to get back to any ship and sail out of sight. If he came in a ship it should be still in view. The discoverer of the footprints climbs a tree from which he can view the sea around the entire island. He can sight no vessel. The supposition or hypothesis that the unknown came in a ship is abandoned. Then the suggestion comes that the unknown has been on the island during the entire time that the shipwrecked man thought himself alone. This suggestion is tested in a manner similar to the others. . . .

The example sums up roughly the general process of all thought, and brings out the motive and value of observation. Let us analyze it.

The first thing to happen is the arousal of a feeling of perplexity, the appearance of a problem. The man has been shambling along, doubtless "thinking" in that loose sense referred to. He has perhaps kicked several stones loose that would have set a geologist worrying, and has picked branches from bushes which would have puzzled a botanist. But this man has not had his curiosity aroused until he has come to these footprints. His thinking starts with his perplexity. After this doubt has been aroused the most obvious solution suggests itself—"my own footprints." But if true, this suggestion involves the co-existence of other facts, some of which are known and some of which may be determined. Thus, *if* they were his own footprints, it must, among other things, necessarily follow (1) that he had been at that spot before, (2) that nothing had happened since that time to remove the prints, (3) that the footprints corresponded to his own. The first consequence involved—that he had been there before—was a fact, but the others were not, and so the suggestion was dropped. Then a second hypothesis occurred

—"the man came in a ship"—and this was tried out in a similar way. Notice that in each case the consequences dependent on the truth of the suggestion are tried out (1) by memory, (2) by observation or experiment. Memory came when he thought of the last time he had walked near the beach and of yesterday's storm. Observation came when he compared his footprint with the one seen, when he followed the footprints along the sand and noticed where they led, when he climbed a tree and looked for a ship. There were a number of other things which he could have observed. He might have noticed the texture of the sand, what kind of a tree he was climbing, what sort of clouds were in the sky. But he did not observe these interesting things simply because they would throw no light on the truth or falsity of his supposition. In another problem one of these facts might have been of value.

It is almost possible to sum up the whole process of thinking as the occurrence of suggestions for the solution of difficulties and the testing out of those suggestions. The suggestions or suppositions are tested by observation,

memory, experiment. Supposition and observation alternate. The first facts observed—in
the case foregoing, the footprints—make the
problem, they suggest the supposition. A supposition is that the man came in a boat. *If*
the man came in a boat such and such would
be the case—the boat would still be visible, etc.
If the boat is not visible the supposition is given
up and another one made; if the boat is visible
the supposition is confirmed. This is a case of
simple and rudimentary thinking, but it illus-
trates roughly the process of thought on even
the most complicated problems of science. The
methods we have been discussing may all be
considered simply as means for helping good
suggestions occur to us.

Let us illustrate by considering a few
methods of rather restricted application. We
are often aided in the solution of a problem by
asking its opposite. If we ask ourselves
"What constitutes gracefulness?" we may find
ourselves at a loss for suggestions, because
gracefulness always seems "so natural." But
if we ask its opposite, "What constitutes awk-

wardness?," suggestions are more apt to occur. If we find, for instance, that awkwardness consists in undue bodily effort in making a movement, we may assume that gracefulness consists in ease of movement. In the same way the question of what makes us forget may be helped by asking ourselves what makes us remember, and light may be thrown on the causes of success in business and in life by a study of the causes of failure.

The method of analogy likewise encourages suggestions. Analogy consists in noting certain likenesses between things, and assuming that they also possess other common qualities. Striking use of analogy is made in dealing with the planet Mars. At each pole there are great white patches. The size of these varies markedly with the seasons, which suggests that like the earth, Mars has great areas of ice and snow at its two poles which melt and re-form. The general surface is reddish, but three-eighths of it is covered by blue-green tracts, and these are usually inferred to be seas. These again are connected by an intricate system of blue-green lines, which some scientists believe to be canals, but on this there is much controversy.   In Mars we have at once an illustration of the possibilities and dangers of analogy.

In the whole discussion of constructive method thus far, I have left out the two most common and useful methods of all.   The first of these we may designate by a somewhat formidable title: *empirical observation.*   Empirical, at least for our present purposes, means merely that which comes within experience.   But the term is generally opposed to scientific.   Thus Dewey gives an example: "A says, 'It will probably rain to-morrow.'   B asks, 'Why do you think so?'   And A replies, 'Because the sky was lowering at sunset.'   When B asks, 'What has that to do with it?' A responds, 'I do not know, but it generally does rain after such a sunset.'   He does not perceive any *connection* between the appearance of the sky and the coming rain; he is not aware of any continuity in the facts themselves—any law or principle, as we usually say.   He simply, from frequently recurring conjunction of the events, has associated them so that when he sees one he thinks of the other."[5]

This, however, is not what I mean to imply by the term empirical observation. I mean rather thinking on the basis merely of facts which occur in the natural course of events, which have not been systematically produced by ourselves or others for the purpose of solving a problem. Logicians usually call this method simply *observation,* and oppose it to experiment. But I object to calling this simply observation because experiment itself is really observation, only in one case we observe merely events which happen to occur, and in the other we observe the results of events *which we have made occur.* The true way of distinguishing these two methods would be to call one *empirical observation,* and the other *experimental observation.*

This empirical method—if indeed I am justified in calling it a *method*—is the most common in all thinking. To give examples of it would be to show how men generally think. But the method has real value, and may even

[5] *How We Think.*

be the most important of all, for if we thought without it our ideas would doubtless be original, but very dangerous. Let us apply it to some of the problems considered under other methods.

Empirical observation is used where experiment is impossible—often, unfortunately, where experiment is merely inconvenient. In political science the empirical method would consist in noting the effect of certain laws,—e. g., tariffs of different countries and of the same country at different periods—and noting economic conditions at the time the different tariffs were in effect. Allowance would be made for other factors which could influence the country's economic condition and the effect of the tariff could then be determined.

The empirical method of dealing with meteorology, the science of weather, would consist in making a study of cloud formations, wind velocity, moisture in the air, temperature, etc., and noting what conditions usually or perhaps invariably followed certain of these conditions. From this, conclusions could be drawn as to what weather to expect following certain conditions.

But valuable as empirical observation is, and often as we must use it, it should never be employed when we can experiment. When the empirical method is rightly used allowance always has to be made for certain irrelevant factors. But "making allowances" is always sheer guess work. *The experimental method consists not in making allowances for certain factors, but in eliminating those factors.* In our example from political science experiment is practically impossible, because the factors which may influence economic conditions are innumerable, and even were they few, no country could survive the dangers of being experimented upon —to say nothing of its permitting it. Experiment is similarly impossible in dealing with weather conditions directly. It is impossible in astronomy.

But it could be applied quite easily to most questions. Suppose you wanted to determine beyond question which of two methods of teaching a given subject was the better. We shall assume for the moment that you have unlimited time and money to experiment. It may be thought that we could settle this simply by teaching one person according to one method and another person according to the other, and that we could determine the relative merits of each method from the progress made by each pupil. This, however, would be practically of no use whatever. One pupil might be naturally brighter than the other, and so would naturally learn quicker, even were he taught by an inferior method.

To make the experiment of any use we should first take two *groups* of pupils—the larger the better. For it is obvious that if we take a great number of pupils and place them in two groups the differences between the individuals will tend to offset one another. Let us say the subject is one in which the progress can be quantitatively measured, say typewriting, and let us suppose there are fifty pupils in each group. If after a given time *all* the pupils in one group had attained a greater speed with accuracy than *all* the pupils in the other, the test would be almost unquestionable. This would be even more conclusive if the groups were reasonably well balanced. For if all of one group were men and all of the other were boys, the men might make more rapid progress than the boys even with a less efficient system. But it should be easy to divide classes and groups so as to have a reasonable balance of intelligence between them. The probable result of any experiment would be that in neither class would all the pupils make more progress than all the pupils of the other, though you might find that the preponderating majority in one class improved faster than those in the other, and this would probably be sufficient to indicate the superiority of one method, even though one or two pupils in the second group progressed faster than one or two in the first.

I say "probably" because there are still many irrelevant factors which might influence the result. For instance, if you had a different teacher for each group, one group might make greater progress not because of the method but because of the teacher. This means either that one teacher should teach both groups, or that we should multiply the number of groups and the number of teachers, and have half the teachers teaching half the groups by one method, and the other half teaching by the other method. Of course here too the more we could multiply the number the better it would be. Even then there might be some reasonable question as to the validity of the experiment, for it might be that one method would tend to encourage faster progress at the beginning, but that the other would lead to greater progress in the long run. This could be determined only by carrying our experiment over a long period. And we might still have irrelevant factors, for the machines on which one group learnt to typewrite might be superior to those on which the other group learnt, and this factor would have to be eliminated in a similar way to the others.

The experimental method has been well summed up by Thomson and Tait in their *Natural Philosophy*:

"In all cases when a particular agent or cause is to be studied, experiments should be arranged in such a way as to lead if possible to results depending on it alone; or, if this cannot be done, they should be arranged so as to increase the effects due to the cause to be studied till these so far exceed the unavoidable concomitants, that the latter may be considered as only disturbing, not essentially modifying the effects of the principal agent.''

In all experiments one must exercise ingenuity in finding other causes besides the one to be studied which may possibly influence a result, and in eliminating these. It might benefit the reader considerably if he were to think out for himself how he would apply experiment in its most thoroughgoing form to solve a given question, say the inheritance of acquired characteristics.

I have now cited enough methods to at least indicate what ''thinking with method'' means. To satisfy a certain human craving all of these have been named, though sometimes arbitrarily. Of course each may have to be modified to some extent to adjust it to different problems. I must repeat: there are methods numberless, and some problems will require methods all their own.

But what is important is that every problem

should be dealt with by as many methods as possible. Doubtless you have used, at some time or other in the course of your thinking, nearly every one of the methods I have so far suggested. But the point is not that you have never used these methods at all, but that you have not used them often enough. You were unaware what method you were using. Consequently you used it only occasionally. You used it only when you stumbled on it accidentally. To formulate methods is to bring them to your attention, so that you may use them always, thoroughly, correctly, consistently.

We have treated political science from most angles. We have applied more than one method to several other problems. To still further clarify, exemplify and impress this point, I shall show the application of method to one more subject.

Suppose you wanted to invent a system of shorthand, and wanted to make it as perfect as possible. How would you go about it?

Your first step should be to restate your question most advantageously. You want to create certain characters or symbols, which will (1) take the shortest time to write, (2) will be easily recognized by yourself or others, even if written carelessly, and (3) which will not be so numerous or so complex as to be difficult to learn. You may decide that such symbols would have even further requirements. Next you should decide on the methods to use in attacking your problem—this in order not to forget any. Now assume you have decided on these methods and that the first is the a priori. Your conclusion might be that it would be impossible to have a different symbol for every word, and that it is necessary to have some sort of alphabet. Should this alphabet be based on that used in longhand? That is, should merely a simpler symbol stand in place of each letter? Or should a different symbol represent each sound? Or would it be possible to have a different elementary symbol for each syllable? Having decided the basis for your symbols or characters, you will know at least approximately the number required. Your problem will then become that of making the characters as simple as possible, so that they may be written most quickly; and yet as different from each other as possible so that if written carelessly (as they will be when written swiftly), they may be easily recognized. You might try writing down all the simplest symbols you can think of. Or you might ask yourself whether there is any fundamental geometrical figure from which you can derive your symbols. Or you might study the simplest and easiest movements of the hand, and base your characters on these.

This a priori method is most apt of all to provoke real thinking. It should therefore be taken up before any of the others. Not only is it best for making you think deeply, but it will be more likely than any of the others to make you think originally. However, whether attended by great or little success, this method should be followed by others.

Not the least fruitful of these would be the evolutionary. This, of course, would consist in studying the history of shorthand, finding out the direction in which it has been tending, and thus anticipating in some degree its future development. As this method is comparative we would naturally be led from it to comparing the shorthand systems of to-day, and assaying the good and bad qualities of each. These could only be assayed if we knew something of shorthand theory, and thus our experience with the deductive or a priori method would be of service.

Implied in here is a method of different nature than any we have yet discussed, but one of immense help. In turning from the deductive method to a study of shorthand systems which others have developed, you have an opportunity to compare the results of your own thinking with those obtained by others. If you have failed to solve the question in as good a manner as these others, you can ask yourself wherein and why your own reflections and ingenuity fell short. If you follow this method with all problems—i.e., thinking a thing out for yourself before looking up what others have thought—you will soon improve your thinking surprisingly. The method is capable of application in every problem, from inventing an adding machine to trying to find how the plumber got that $3.46 on the bill.

But to return to shorthand. We still have

the empirical and experimental methods. In
this particular case the difference between them
would be simply one of degree. We could find,
for instance, what systems were used by the
fastest shorthand writers; but we could get
nothing conclusive from this, for we would have
to make allowance for the natural ability and
length of training of these writers. From
merely looking at two outlines or characters, it
is often difficult to tell which can be written
faster. This could only be tested by writing
hundreds in a row and finding the time it took
to write the same number of each. Of course
such experiment is capable of indefinite expan-
sion.

In dealing with method heretofore, I have at
times come dangerously near to making a false
assumption. I have been talking as if a man
who took up political science, shorthand, or any
other subject, were dealing with only one problem. As a matter of fact he is dealing with a
whole series of problems. Just how many it is
difficult to say, because no problem worthy of
the name is an indivisible unit, and may always
be broken into smaller problems. The whole

science of æsthetics is included in the simple
question "What is beauty?", the science of
ethics is merely the answer to "What is right
conduct?", and metaphysics may be reduced to
the problem "What is reality?" But when we
come to deal with any of these we instinctively
break them up into smaller and more concrete
problems, making the treatment easier, just as a
general attempts to split his enemy's forces, so
that he can annihilate one section at a time.
Often, indeed, the very division of the larger
problem into smaller problems constitutes its
solution, for we finally come to a problem which
practically answers itself, and which we recognize as being included in, or a particular form
of, some more general problem to which we already know the answer.

A man sets before himself the question,
"What is the proper sphere of Government?"
Perhaps he will first of all consider certain different specific activities which might possibly
be supposed to come within the sphere of gov-
ernmental interference. He might ask himself,
for instance, "Should the Government interfere
with freedom of contract?" Notice that he has

here temporarily made his problem narrower, he has chosen to break it up in order to deal with it part by part. But even when he came to cope with this smaller problem he would probably find it necessary to break this up, and he would therefore take a specific example. Suppose a man works for so much an hour, and that nine hours' work a day gives him the minimum amount on which he can live and support his family. Would it be wise to limit the legal working day of such a man to eight hours? This problem practically answers itself, and so further division is unnecessary. Of course the answer to this does not determine the answer to the original question, for other parts still remain to be considered.

In fact, much of the success of our thinking will depend upon just how we divide our big problems into subsidiary problems, and just what our subsidiary or subordinate problems are. This will depend to some extent on our own natural sagacity, and to some extent on mere chance. No rigid rules can be laid down. The only advice which can be offered is that when a thinker breaks up a problem he should do so with an eye to utility and definiteness.

John Stuart Mill, in an essay on Jeremy Bentham, pointed out that the secret of the latter's strength and originality of thought lay in his method, which "may be shortly described as the method of detail; of treating wholes by separating them into their parts, abstractions by resolving them into things,—classes and generalities by distinguishing them into the individuals of which they are made up; and breaking every question into pieces before attempting to solve it." The method was not absolutely original with Bentham, but "whatever originality there was in the method, in the subjects he applied it to, and in the rigidity with which he adhered to it, there was the greatest."

The systematic thinker is careful of the manner in which he marshals his difficulties. He knows that certain problems should properly be considered before certain others, and he saves himself labor and sometimes error by considering them in that order. Before asking himself how Government should cure a given social evil, he first asks whether it is the duty or even the right of the State to attend to that particular evil at all. In other words, before asking what the State should do in any particular case, he considers first what the proper sphere of government is. It must be admitted that a previous question often cannot be discovered until one has actually attempted the solution of a problem. In the foregoing instance, it would be difficult to determine the proper sphere of government by any other method than a consideration of particular cases where government interference suggests itself.

In fact, it is only by deep reflection on a subject that we come to realize most of the problems involved. You walk along the road with your friend the botanist and he stops to pick what looks to you to be a common wild flower. "Hm," he muses, "I wonder how that got in this part of the country?" Now that is no problem to you, simply because you do not happen to know why that particular flower should *not* be there—and what men do not know about they take for granted. Knowledge furnishes problems, and the discovery of problems itself constitutes an intellectual advance.

Whenever you are thrashing out a subject, write down every problem, difficulty and objection that occurs to you. When you get what you consider a satisfactory solution, see whether or not it answers all of them.

I have stated that method is essential to good thinking. I have given rules and examples of methodic thinking. But I do not want to create a false impression. If a man has not within him the materials of a thinker, no amount of method can make him one. Half the thinking process, as pointed out, depends on the occurrence of suggestions. The occurrence of suggestions depends on how ideas are associated in a man's mind. While this depends to some extent on the education and the whole past life and environment of the individual, it depends far more on inborn mental qualities. All method can do is to awaken the most fruitful associations of ideas already in mind. Hence the more methods we adopt—the greater the number of views we take of any problem—the more solutions will suggest themselves.

There is one further reason why we should take as many different viewpoints as possible.

In our example of the inheritance of acquired characteristics in animals, if we had been sure that the results of our deductive reasoning were correct, it would have been a sinful waste of time to experiment. But when we attack a problem by several methods we can compare the results from each. If these results agree we have good evidence that our solution is correct. But if we have adopted quite a number of viewpoints, and have not let the results of one influence those of the next, they are almost certain to be at variance. This means that we have erred in applying one or several methods. How are we to find which of the methods it was, and how are we to prevent such errors?

This is the subject of our next chapter.

III

A FEW CAUTIONS

THUS far we have considered only positive
and constructive thinking, and means for
obtaining relevant suggestions. We have had
almost nothing to do with cautions, means for
avoiding fallacy and error, and means for testing the truth and value of suggestions. Most
writers who have discussed thinking have dwelt
so much on the negative aspect—so much on
what we should not do—and have so slighted the
question of what we should do, that I have perhaps been led to adopt this order, more from a
feeling of revolt than because it is logically better. But I believe I have logic on my side.
Constructive methods make thinking "go";
cautions steer it in the right path. An automobile without a steering gear is almost as useless
as one without a motor. But an automobile
can go without being steered, whereas it cannot
be steered unless it is going.

But while with automobiles we can clearly divide moving from steering, we cannot do this with thinking. The two processes are so inextricably bound up, that we cannot engage in one without engaging in the other; we cannot even speak of one without implying the other. I have divided them for convenience of exposition. But in the last chapter we were forced to deal slightly with cautions, and here we shall have to consider constructive methods to some extent.

A case in point is classification. In taking this up from a constructive standpoint, I remarked that all classifications ought to be logical. But I did not say what I meant by logical, nor did I tell how a logical classification could be secured. The two most prominent errors made in classifying are (1) not making classifications mutually exclusive, (2) not making them cover all the objects or phenomena supposed to be classified.

The first error is the less common, for though occurring among all thinkers, it is comparatively infrequent among those who proceed with caution. It is, moreover, more easily discov-

ered than the second. Consider the classification of constructive methods into comparison,
observation, and experiment. It is apparent
that these methods overlap. We cannot compare without observing, much of our observation
involves comparison, when we experiment we
must of course observe the results obtained, and
the results are usually always compared. All
three methods could be classed under observation. It is well to remember, however, that the
first classification may be useful—even more so
than one strictly logical, and that the nature of
a subject will often make impracticable, divis-
ions which do not overlap in some degree.

The second error—that of not making a classification cover all the objects or phenomena
it is supposed to cover—is not so easy to detect.
It is one to which the greatest philosophers have
been heir. Some of our Socialist friends say
there are but two kinds of people: capitalists
and laborers, "the people who live on others and
the people who are lived on." They overlook
that class of farmers who own a little piece of
land and do their own tilling. Even if they insist that such a class "is rapidly becoming ex-

tinct,'' the fact remains that it is still with us and must be taken into account.

All classifications are made with a certain number of facts in mind, and fortunate is he who happens to have just the right facts. We cannot hold many facts in mind at once, and we often generalize upon thousands of things by taking a supposedly representative dozen. To avoid error all we can do is to keep constantly on the lookout for examples, especially those which apparently will not fit into our generalization. If they go in without straining anything, our classification receives added warrant. But sometimes you will find that where you have three classes a new fact will necessitate a fourth, and that often it will overturn your whole beautiful structure.

There is another phase of thinking, which while chiefly cautionary, is also in part constructive. We have so often been warned to ''avoid the treachery of words'' and to ''define all our terms'' that a repetition of the advice seems unnecessary. But we cannot overlook the excellent counsel of Blaise Pascal. He urges that we not only define our terms, but that whenever we use them we mentally substitute the definition. However, this needs to be qualified. If every time we used a term we stopped to substitute its definition, our thought might be exact but would hardly move forward very rapidly. It will usually be sufficient simply to substitute the definition a few times, for after doing this we shall gradually come to know exactly what we mean by a term, and further substitution would merely waste time. Of course, all this need be applied only to terms new, technical or equivocal; or those used in a mooted proposition.

I have spoken of analogy as a constructive method. This, however, should be used only for suggestion, for it is most dangerous. Often we use an analogy and are quite unaware of it. Thus many social and political thinkers have called society an "organism," and have proceeded to deal with it as if it were a large animal. They have thought not in terms of the actual phenomena under consideration, but in terms of the analogy. In so far as the terms of the analogy were more concrete than those of the phenomena, their thinking has been made easier. But no analogy will ever hold good throughout, and consequently these thinkers have often fallen into error.

The quickest way to detect error in analogy is to carry it out as far as it will go—and further. Every analogy will break down somewhere. Any analogy if carried out far enough becomes absurd. We are most likely to err when we carry an analogy too far, but not to the point where the absurdity is apparent. Take the analogy employed in our first chapter, comparing thinking and a ship. For the sake of the image I shall make this a motor-boat. We might carry this out further. We might compare the effect on the mind of books and experience to the fuel used for the engine. The brain, transforming outward experience into thought, might be paralleled with a carburetor transforming fuel into usable form. An idea may be compared to a spark. All this is very fascinating. It may even lead to suggestions of real value. But it is bound soon or late to develop into the ludicrous. The analogy in question, however, does not need to be developed to be confuted. For unless a boat has a pro-

peller and a rudder, its engine is useless. A
mind is capable of attaining truth without even
being aware of the existence of a science of
thinking or of logic.

Another way to find whether an analogy is
fallacious is to see whether you can discover a
counter analogy. Surely this is the most effective practice in refuting analogy in argument.
This suggests the case of the man who had a
ticket from New York to Chicago, and tried to
use it from Chicago to New York. The railroad
refused to accept it, whereupon the man brought
suit. The lawyer for the defendant, in the heat
of the debate, said, "Why, a man might just as
well pay for a barrel of potatoes and then demand a barrel of apples!" Whereupon the attorney for the plaintiff replied, "It would be
rather like a grocer selling a man a barrel of
potatoes and then trying to compel him to eat
them from the top down, refusing to allow him to
turn the barrel upside down and begin eating
them from the bottom up." It is best to avoid
analogy except for purposes of suggestion, or
as a rhetorical device for explaining an idea already arrived at by other means.

I have been forced to defend my advice to take as many viewpoints as possible, by pointing out that the conclusions obtained from these viewpoints might disagree; in fact would be almost sure to disagree. Of course, this disagreement might be avoided if we allowed the conclusions reached by one method or viewpoint to influence our conclusions in another. But if we do this we give our problem more shallow treatment, and we are not so sure of a result when we get it. When a mathematician adds a column of figures from the top down, he confirms by re-adding from the bottom up. He knows that if he added in the same manner the second time he would be liable to fall into the same errors. And in thinking, when we leave one method and take up another, we should try to forget entirely the first conclusion and begin on the problem as if we had never taken it up before. After we have taken up all the applicable methods, then, and then only, should we begin to compare conclusions.

Time forbids doing this with all problems. Time forbids even attacking all problems from

different points of view. But there are some
problems where this unquestionably ought to be
done. The problem of whether or not characteristics acquired during the life time of one
individual may be inherited by his offspring, if
dealt with at all, is too important to be left to
the a priori method alone. This problem asks
whether the children of educated parents will
necessarily be innately superior to the children
of uneducated parents; it asks whether the man
of today is superior to the ancient Greek, or
even the present day savage; or, assuming that
the negro race is inferior to the white race, it
asks whether generations of education will
bring it to the white race level or leave it un-
changed; it asks whether the hope of improving
the human race lies in education or eugenics.
No question can be more important than this in
its practical bearings. The answer to it will
profoundly influence our opinions in education,
psychology, ethics, economics, political science
—even philosophy and metaphysics. The answer we obtain to this question from deductive
reasoning, no matter how unanswerable or con-

clusive it may seem, should be checked up by
nothing short of the most thoroughgoing experiment.

Unfortunately the experiments needed for
this particular question cannot be carried on by
the layman. It is equally to be regretted that
scientists have been none too thorough in carrying them out themselves. But we should remember that any result we arrive at should be
subject to revision, and that if we take up this
problem at all, we should at least make it our
duty to read about and criticise all the experiments that come to our notice.

A question has perhaps just occurred to the
reader. If the deductive method is to be
checked up by experiment, and the results of
the experiment are always to be taken, why not
experiment first, and omit theory altogether?

Leaving aside the fact that theory is the best
guide for experiment—that were it not for
theory and the problems and hypotheses that
come out of it, we would not know the points we
wanted to verify, and hence would experiment
aimlessly—a more serious objection is that experiment is seldom if ever perfect, for it nearly

always involves some unverified assumption. I
have referred to empirical observation and experiment as two different methods. But the
difference is mainly, if not solely, one of degree.
If we experimented to find out whether acquired characteristics were inherited, it is obvious that our experiments would have to be confined to animals. If we found, let us say, that
no acquired characteristic was ever transmitted
to offspring, we could not say that this would
be equally true of man, but would be justified in
concluding only that the acquired characteristics of *animals* are not transmitted to descend-
ants. Nay, we could not go even this far. We
would have to confine ourselves to the statement
that certain acquired characteristics of the few
score animals we had experimented upon were
not transmissible. But even this statement
would involve assumption. We could say only
that certain acquired characteristics of the few
score animals we had experimented upon had
not been transmitted in these particular instances. We would have to limit ourselves to a
bare statement of fact; we could draw no conclusion whatever. But if we had attacked this

problem from the deductive standpoint, and had concluded that owing to certain conditions holding alike in all animals and in man, acquired characteristics *could not possibly* be transmitted, we would have sufficient ground for deriving from our experiments a broad generalization.

Experiment and deduction are not the only methods which can be checked up against each other. We can do likewise with the comparative and the experimental, the historical and the theoretical—in fact, all viewpoints applicable to any one problem.

When you encounter a question about which there is a controversy, and where the adherents of both sides nearly equal each other in number and intellectual status, you may be almost certain that each side has caught sight of some truth, but that neither has seen the whole truth; and you should endeavor to unite both sides by a broader and deeper solution. A classic philosophical example of this method is Herbert Spencer's attempt to reconcile science and religion, and his effort to unite the "intuitional" and "experiential" schools of thought. The intuitionists maintained that the mind had from birth intuitions by which it knew certain truths independently of experience. Such truths as the axiom that a straight line is the shortest distance between two points, or that it is morally wrong to do certain acts, were regarded as among these intuitions. The "empiricists" or "sensationalists," on the other hand, maintained that all our knowledge—even of such a fact, for instance, as that two and two are four, where we cannot conceive otherwise—is learned solely from the individual's experience, taken in its broadest sense. Herbert Spencer thought he recognized some truth in both these doctrines, and came forward with the theory that there are certain truths which are intuitions so far as the individual is concerned, but that these intuitions have been inherited from our ancestors, were originally built up through the ages, and represent the accumulated experience of the race. Whatever may be thought of Spencer's success in this case, the value of the method itself is undoubted. It was frequently used by Kant, Hegel, Fichte and other German philosophers.

I have remarked that it is almost possible to sum up the entire process of thinking as the occurrence of suggestions for the solution of difficulties and the testing out of those suggestions. The constructive methods discussed were called means for making good suggestions occur to us. From this standpoint the cautions with which we have just been dealing may be considered as tests of suggestions.

Let us refer back to the analysis of thinking given in the case of the man who discovered footprints on the beach. Even there, in order to give any adequate idea of his thought process, I was obliged to show that for various reasons he rejected certain suggested solutions. But this negative method could be more fully developed. Because the man rejected a certain solution, it does not follow that it was necessarily wrong. Suppose the final suggestion—that the unknown had been on the island all the time—were to have been tested out, and that certain further facts were discovered which tended

to disprove it; the man might find it necessary
to look for still another solution.   But suppose
this were not forthcoming, suppose that all the
possibilities had been exhausted.   It would be
necessary to return to some of the original
suggestions.   He would have to see whether an
error had been made in testing them.   In rejecting the suggestion of a small boat he may
have overestimated the distance of this island
from other land.   He may have underestimated
the difficulties that a man in a small boat is
capable of surmounting.   In rejecting the supposition of a ship, he may have erred in his
judgment of the time the footprints had been on
the beach, or of the time it would take a large
vessel to get out of sight.

What is essential is that all suggestions be
tested out, either by memory, observation or
experiment, in all their implications, and that
the tendency be resisted to accept the first solution that suggests itself.   For the uncritical
thinker will always jump at the first suggestion,
unless an objection actually forces itself into
view.   Remaining in a state of doubt is unpleasant.   The longer the doubt remains the

more unpleasant it becomes. But the man who is willing to accept this unpleasantness, the man who is willing carefully to observe, or experiment if need be, to test the validity of his suggestions, will finally arrive at a solution much deeper, and one which will give him far more satisfaction, than the superficial answer obtained by the man of careless habits of thought.

Thomas A. Edison says he always rejects an easy solution of any problem and looks for something difficult. But the inventor has one great advantage over any other kind of thinker. He can test his conclusion in a tangible way. If his device works, his thinking was right; if his device doesn't work, his thinking was wrong. But the philosopher, the scientist, the social reformer, has no such satisfactory test. His only satisfaction is the feeling that his results harmonize with all his experience. The more critical he has been in arriving at those results, the more deep and permanent will be that feeling, the more valuable will be his thoughts to himself and to the world. . . ..

Even in the first chapter I intimated that logic

would constitute a part of the science of thinking. I intimated, moreover, that it would constitute almost the whole of what may be called the negative side of thinking—those rules which serve to steer thought aright. Though cautionary, the advice given in this chapter is not usually given in books on logic. But though I cannot overemphasize the importance of a knowledge of logic, I cannot deal with it here. The science can receive justice only in a book devoted entirely to it.

If he has not already done so the would-be thinker should study a work on logic, for unless the present book is supplemented by some treatise on that science it cannot be regarded as complete.

In order not to confuse the reader I shall recommend only one book. In order to encourage him I shall recommend a small book, one not so deep as to be incomprehensible or repulsive to the beginner, but at the same time one which is recognized as a standard treatise:—*Elementary Lessons in Logic,* by Stanley Jevons.

IV

CONCENTRATION

What is the hardest task in the world? To think.
—EMERSON.

WE have been dealing with the subject of thinking. We have considered it from both a positive and negative side. But while we have devoted our attention to thinking, we have neglected the thinker. In more scientific terms, we have treated thought from the logical side; we are now to treat it from the psychological.

Few people will admit specific faults in themselves of any kind, especially if these happen to be intellectual. But almost any man is willing to confess that he cannot always "concentrate" when he wants to, in fact, that he is one of the countless victims of "mind wandering."

Most of us imagine we know just what we mean by both these terms. But if we are to judge by most of what has been written, no two terms are more misconceived. Before trying to find the best means of concentrating, we must first find just what we mean by concentration.

In a previous chapter I said that suggestions for solutions "occurred." I did not say how or why. To discover this we must refer to the famous psychological principle of association.

Any train of thought is made possible by previous connections of ideas in our minds. While a girl sits at her window a parade passes along a nearby street. The band is playing, and ere the tune is completed the band has gone so far that the music is no longer audible. But the tune still goes along in her mind, and she completes it herself. It suggests a dance she had been to where it was played, and this suggests that she danced the two-step to it. The two-step suggests the more modern one-step, and this leads her to compare the familiar dancing of to-day with the distant and respectful minuet.

This is an example of a random train of ideas. It is that loose "thinking" referred to in our first chapter. But even this is made possible only by the connection of ideas in our mind at some previous period. No thought can enter our minds unless it is associated in some way with the previous thought. Psychologists have traditionally classified associations into four kinds: association by succession, by contiguity, by similarity and by contrast. The example just given involves all four. Association by succession means that when two ideas or impressions of objects have entered the mind in succession, the second is likely to be suggested whenever the first is thought of. A tune consists in a succession of notes, and when the first notes are brought to mind, as by a passing band, the rest will follow—sometimes in spite of ourselves. Association by contiguity means that when two objects or ideas have been in consciousness together, one is always likely to suggest the other thereafter. This was the case with the music and the dance, or the music and the two-step. Association by similarity occurs when two ideas resemble each other in some particular. They need not have occurred together at any past time, nor after each other. The fact that they have a common element suffices to bring up one idea when the other is in mind: thus the two-step suggested the one-step. Association by contrast needs no explanation. It is exemplified when the idea of present-day dancing brings up the idea of distant dancing.

Any attempt to show *why* the mind acts in this way, any explanation of the way in which the different kinds of association are made possible, would bring us into physiological psychology, would involve a study of the brain and the nervous system. For our purposes it is sufficient to keep in mind that such associations do take place. Without them no idea can occur. Without them thought is impossible.

The bearing of all this on concentration has yet to be made plain. We must remember that every idea has more than one associate; in fact that each idea generally has a cluster of possible associates. Instead of suggesting the minuet, the one-step may have made the fox trot or the three-step occur to the young lady. It may have made her think of a young man with whom she danced it, or the trouble she had in learning it. Each of these suggestions, in turn, would also have potential connections with a cluster of ideas. When we are thinking at random—when we are day dreaming, as in the example given—the strongest association, or the first to be aroused, is the one we dwell upon. But when we are thinking with a purpose, in a word, when we are reasoning, we reject all associations which have no bearing on our purpose, and select only those which serve it.

Concentration does not, as popularly supposed, mean keeping the mind fastened on one object or idea or in one place. It consists in having a problem or purpose constantly before one. It means keeping our thought moving toward one desired end.

Concentration is often regarded as intense or focused attention. But the fact is that all attention is focused attention. Psychologists are fairly well agreed that we can attend to only one thing at a time. Mind wandering, and so-called distributed attention, is really attention directed first to one thing, then to another, then to another; or first to one thing, then to another, and then back again to the original object, resting but a few moments on each idea.

Concentration may best be defined as prolonged or sustained attention. It means keeping the mind on one subject or problem for a relatively long period, or at least continually reverting to some problem whenever one's thoughts momentarily leave it.

Having decided just what we mean by concentration, our next step is to inquire whether concentration is worth while. The reader may smile at this question or he may be shocked, according to his temperament. But if most men were so convinced that concentration is such an unquestionable virtue, they would practice it a little more. At least they would make greater efforts to practice it than they do at present.

The truth is that concentration, *per se,* is of little value. The value of concentration depends almost entirely on the subject concentrated on. Almost any one will agree that even were a man to allow his mind to dwell now on one important problem and now on another, without stopping a very appreciable time at any, he might nevertheless be improving his time far more than a man who concentrated continually on some insignificant and inconsequential question.

But of course this is not really an argument against concentration. It has no application when you concentrate on the proper subject. For if you start to concentrate on some question which you have decided is really important, you should keep at it, allowing no deviation. It may be that during the course of your thought associations will be aroused which will suggest or bear upon important problems, problems more important perhaps than the one you originally started to concentrate on. But if you immediately abandoned every problem you started to think of, whenever you came across one which you imagined was just as important, you would probably never really solve any big question.

Our attention is guided by interest. If a man merely allows his thoughts to flow at random, thinking only of those things which spontaneously arouse his interest, he may or may not attend to things worth thinking about. All will depend upon the path in which his natural interests run. But the point is that if the subject he thinks about is valuable, it will be so only by accident; whether or not his thinking is useful will depend upon mere chance. If however he consciously chooses a subject—chooses it because he believes it to be important—then his thinking will be worth while.

But there is another reason why concentration is necessary. Suppose a man started to put up a barbed wire fence, got as far as driving in all the posts, then lost interest in the fences and decided to grow potatoes in his field, plowed up the ground, lost interest in the field and neglected to plant the seeds; decided to paint his house, got the porch done, lost interest . . . That man might work as hard as any other man, but he would never get anything done. So with the mind wanderer and the concentrator. The mind wanderer thinks of a problem, loses interest, and abandons it. The concentrator sticks to it until it is solved.

Much of our mind wandering is due to the fact that we are not fully convinced of the importance of the problem being attacked, or that we regard other problems or ideas as more important. Concentration consists in devoting one's mind to the solution of one problem. During our train of thought associations bring up new ideas or suggest problems which do not bear on the question at hand. Now when we wander, when we follow up these irrelevant ideas or suggested problems, or when we happen to glance at something or hear something and begin to think of that, we do so because of a half-conscious belief that the new idea, problem or fact needs attending to, is important. I have already pointed out that if this new idea is important it will be so only by accident. If we were consciously to ask ourselves whether any of these irrelevant problems were as important as the one we were concentrating on, or even important at all, we would find, nine times out of ten, that they were not.

Therefore before beginning to concentrate you should assure yourself that the problem you are about to attack is one worth solving, or at least devoting a certain time to. And during that time you should think only of that problem, and unhesitatingly throw out all irrelevant suggestions coming either from your course of thought or from external sights and sounds.

One qualification is necessary. Sometimes an irrelevant suggestion occurs which is nevertheless really important and worth developing. As this might be forgotten, and as it might never occur again, it would be poor counsel indeed to ask that it be thrown aside forever. The best move in such a case would be to make written note of the suggestion or problem, so that it could be referred to at some future time. Having written the idea, you will have it off your mind, and will be able to continue your line of thought without perturbation.

It has been suggested that a great aid to concentration is writing one's thoughts. It must be admitted that this certainly helps one to keep much closer to a subject. Ordinarily we wander without being aware of it, and bring our minds back to a subject only after sudden intermittent realizations that we have gone astray. When we write our thoughts, however, we doubly secure ourselves against mind wandering. All writing requires a certain effort, and this alone is sufficient to keep most of us from writing irrelevant thoughts, or anything not directly bearing upon the subject in hand.

When we write, too, we capture our thoughts in tangible symbols; we make them less elusive than in their original form. Finally, we keep our entire past train of thought in view. Like an oarsman, who cannot look ahead, but guides himself by the objects he is constantly leaving further behind, we keep to our original course of thought by a survey of the ideas already written.

In spite of these great advantages, writing has certain serious handicaps as a practical method for concentrating. First among these is its slowness. Thoughts flash through our minds much faster than we can write them. We either lose many ideas by the wayside, or fail to go as far in our subject as we otherwise would. Another disadvantage is that we are forced to give part of our attention to the physical act of writing, and thus cannot concentrate entirely on our subject.

There are two methods of writing comparatively free of at least one of these handicaps. Both shorthand and typewriting, if mastered to any degree, are much faster than ordinary writing. This is especially true, of course, of shorthand. But even with a good stenographer shorthand has serious defects. Unless one is quite expert it requires even more attention than longhand, and at that is often unable to keep pace with thought. Typewriting requires almost no attention from a touch operator, but it too is open to the charge of slowness, coming in this respect about midway between short and longhand.

But to those so unfortunate as not to know either shorthand or typewriting the necessity for still another method is evident. Indeed, even those acquainted with these two arts cannot always use them. If every time we were to think we had to have with us a typewriter, or even a pencil and note-book, we would not engage in any too much reflection.

Fortunately there is one method superior to any yet named, which requires no study before its application, and no paraphernalia during it. It consists in simply talking your thoughts as you think them. One who has not tried this can have no idea of its effect. It possesses almost all the advantages of writing. You cannot wander without realizing the fact immediately.

It makes your thinking much less vague than if you thought silently, increases your vocabulary, always keeps pace with your ideas, and requires practically no attention.

It may be objected that silent thinking itself is put in unspoken words. But this is not true. Part of silent thinking consists of unspoken words, but part of it consists of images, concepts and attitudes which pass through our minds and which we do not take the trouble to name. In silent thinking, too, there are also what appear to be occasional dead stops. All these processes drift into each other indefinably and are unrecognizable. When we talk we realize whether our images or concepts are vague or definite by our ability to name them, and we realize when our thought comes to a "dead stop" by the fact that we miss the sound of our own voice.

Another practice can be used with talking. The degree of concentration we give to any subject depends upon the degree of natural interest we take in it. Mind wandering comes because we are also interested in other subjects. No matter how slight our interest in a thing, we would always concentrate on it if we were interested in nothing else. To secure sustained attention, then, we should (1) stimulate or increase interest in problems we want to concentrate on, (2) decrease or remove temporarily any interest in the things we do not want to think about. Men often complain that noises distract their attention. While not impossible, it is inconvenient and unpleasant to shut off our ears. But men are far more distracted by sights than they are by sounds. And they never think of merely shutting their eyes. The next time you attempt to concentrate—silently or by talking—try shutting your eyes and see whether or not you are helped.

Talking has one disadvantage—it cannot always be used. To practice it, you must either lock yourself up in your room, or sit alone in a forest or field, or walk along unfrequented streets and by-ways. You can by no means allow any one to hear or see you talking to yourself. If you are caught doing this some asinine idiot is sure to mistake you for one.

We are brought back again, then, to the necessity of occasionally thinking in silence. There is one other reason why we shall sometimes need to do this. Thoughts of certain kinds are so elusive that to attempt to articulate them is to scare them away, as a fish is scared by the slightest ripple. When these thoughts are in embryo, even the infinitesimal attention required for talking cannot be spared. But later, as they take more definite and coherent form, they can and should be put into words, for otherwise they will be incommunicable and useless.

No definite rule can be laid down, however, as to what should be spoken and what thought of silently. This depends to a large extent upon the individual thinker. Some will probably find that talking helps them in almost all their thinking, others that it is often an actual hindrance. The same is true of closing one's eyes. If you do not know which is better for you, find out by experiment.

At those times when you suddenly catch yourself wandering, it would be a good plan to stop occasionally and trace back your train of thought to the point where it left its original direction. In this way you would get some valuable insight into the *how* and *why* of mind wandering; you would be helped in recognizing its appearance sooner the next time it occurred.

Whenever a person is left alone for a short time, with no one to talk to and no "reading matter"; when for instance, he is standing at a station waiting for his train, or sitting at a restaurant table waiting for his order, or hanging on a subway strap when he has forgotten to buy a newspaper, his "thoughts" tend to run along the tracks they have habitually taken. If a young man usually allows a popular tune to float through his head, that will be most likely to happen; if he usually thinks of that young lady, he will most likely think of her then; if he has often imagined himself as some great political orator making a speech amid the plaudits of the multitude, he is likely to see a mental picture of himself swinging his arms, waving flags and gulping water.

The only way a man can put a stop to such pleasant but uneducative roamings, is to snap off his train of day dreaming the first moment he becomes aware of it, and to address his mind to some useful serious subject. His thoughts will be almost sure to leak away again. They may do this as often as fifteen times in half an hour. But the second he becomes aware of it he should dam up the stream and send his thoughts along the channel he has laid out for them. If he has never done this he will find the effort great. But if he merely resolves now that the next time his mind wanders he will stop it in this manner, his resolve will tend to make itself felt. If he succeeds in following this practice once it will be much easier a second time. Every time he does this it will become increasingly easy, until he will have arrived at the point where his control over his thoughts will be almost absolute. Not only will it be increasingly easy for him to turn his mind to serious subjects. It will become constantly more pleasurable. Frivolous and petty trains of thought will become more and more intolerable.

This whole idea of forcing our thought has been questioned by no less a thinker than Herbert Spencer. Let us hear what he has to say regarding his own practice:

"It has never been my way to set before myself a problem and puzzle out an answer. The conclusions at which I have from time to time arrived, have not been arrived at as solutions of questions raised; but have been arrived at unawares—each as the ultimate outcome of a body of thoughts which slowly grew from a germ. Some direct observation, or some fact met with in reading, would dwell with me: apparently because I had a sense of its significance. It was not that there arose a distinct consciousness of its general meaning; but rather that there was a kind of instinctive interest in those facts which have general meanings. For example, the detailed structure of this or that species of mammal, though I might willingly read about it, would leave little impression; but when I met with the statement that, almost without exception, mammals, even as unlike as the whale and the giraffe, have seven cervical vertebræ, this would strike me and be remembered as suggestive. Apt as I thus was to lay hold of cardinal truths, it would happen occasionally that one, most likely brought to mind by an illustration, and gaining from the illustration fresh distinctiveness, would be contemplated by me for a while, and its bearings observed. A week afterwards, possibly, the matter would be remembered; and with further thought about it, might occur a recognition of some wider application than I had before perceived: new instances being aggregated with those already noted. Again after an interval, perhaps of a month, perhaps of half a year, something would remind me of that which I had before remarked; and mentally running over the facts might be followed by some further extension of the idea. When accumulation of instances had given body to a generalization, reflexion would reduce the vague conception at first framed to a more definite conception; and perhaps difficulties or anomalies passed over for a while, but eventually forcing themselves on attention, might cause a needful qualification and a truer shaping of the thought. Eventually the growing generalization, thus far inductive, might take a deductive form: being all at once recognized as a necessary consequence of some physical principle—some established law. And thus, little by little, in unobtrusive ways, without conscious intention or appreciable effort, there would grow up a coherent and organized theory. Habitually the process was one of slow unforced 'development, often extending over years; and the thinking done went on in this gradual, almost spontaneous way, without strain. . . ."[1]

But compare this method with that of John Stuart Mill; who speaks of "the mental habit to which I attribute all that I have ever done, or ever shall do, in speculation; that of never abandoning a puzzle, but again and again returning to it until it was cleared up; never allowing obscure corners of a subject to remain unexplored because they did not appear important; never thinking that I perfectly understood any part of a subject until I understood the whole."[2] Mill's method was, in short, "that of conscious and vehement effort directed towards the end he had in view. He solved his problems by laborious application and study."[3]

William Minto writes of Adam Smith: "His intellectual proceedings were calm, patient, and regular: he mastered a subject slowly and circumspectly, and carried his principles with steady tenacity through multitudes of details

[1] *Autobiography*, Vol. I, p. 463.
[2] *Autobiography*.
[3] Hugh Elliot, *The Letters of John Stuart Mill*.

that would have checked many men of greater mental vigor unendowed with the same invincible persistence.''

With such thinkers differing so markedly in their methods, the ordinary man is left bewildered. He may indeed decide that effort or no effort makes little difference. Let us, however, look to the psychology of the question, and see whether we can find any guiding principle.

Spencer, defending his method, says: ''A solution reached in the way described, is more likely to be true than one reached in pursuance of a determined effort to find a solution. The determined effort causes perversion of thought. When endeavoring to recollect some name or thing which has been forgotten, it frequently happens that the name or thing sought will not arise in consciousness; but when attention is relaxed, the missing name or thing often suggests itself. While thought continues to be forced down certain wrong turnings which had originally been taken, the search is vain; but with the cessation of strain the true association of ideas has an opportunity of asserting itself. And, similarly, it may be that while an effort to ar-

rive forthwith at some answer to a problem,
acts as a distorting factor in consciousness and
causes error, a quiet contemplation of the problem from time to time, allows those proclivities
of thought which have probably been caused unawares by experiences, to make themselves felt,
and to guide the mind to the right conclusion.''

Spencer's first argument, that an effort to
recollect something is often without results,
while the thing is remembered later when we
are not trying to think of it, is true as to fact.
But it does not show that the effort was un-
fruitful. As pointed out in the discussion of
association, one idea is associated with not only
one other idea but with an entire group. This
may give a possible explanation of why it is so
often difficult to recollect anything when we
make a determined effort. The attempt partly
arouses a whole cluster of ideas, each of which
tends to return, but is prevented from doing so
by all the others. It is analogous to a crowd of
people all struggling to get through a narrow
doorway. They cause such a jam that for a
time no one succeeds. When the pushing and
jostling cease one person at a time is able to

pass through. When effort is abandoned, probably all but one of the associates become dormant, and this one slides into consciousness at the slightest provocation.

Whether or not this explanation is true, it is a fact that though an effort may not produce results at the time, still if it had not been made, the associate which finally comes to mind would probably never have occurred at all. The reader has possibly found that when learning some skilled movement, such as bicycle riding, skating or swimming, his first attempts seemed without result, but after an interval of a week or a month, when trying again, he suddenly discovered that he could do what he wanted from the very start. Surely no one would contend that this could happen without the previous effort!

I must also question Spencer's remark that "with the cessation of strain the true association of ideas has an opportunity of asserting itself." The brain has no hidden mechanism by which it can separate the true from the false. To be sure, if we use no effort the most usual and strongest associations will be more likely to assert themselves, and it may be that often these will have more warrant than unusual and weaker associations. Outside of this, there is no superiority.

But the main reason why we cannot follow the method of Herbert Spencer is that we are not all Herbert Spencers. His thought naturally tended to serious and useful channels. Consequently he did not have to force it there. If the reader is one of those rare and fortunate beings whose thoughts run only to useful subjects, and who always concentrate from pure spontaneous interest, I sincerely advise him not to force himself. And if such a being happens to be reading the present chapter I assure him he is criminally wasting his time, and that he should drop the book or turn to the next chapter with all possible haste. But if the reader numbers himself with the miserable majority whose minds are ever running away with them, he will find it necessary to use effort in thinking—at least for a while.

One remark of Spencer is undoubtedly true. This is "that an effort to arrive forthwith at some answer to a problem, acts as a distorting

factor in consciousness and causes error."
And here, strange to say, his practice is in substantial agreement with the apparently opposite method of John Stuart Mill. For note that Mill speaks of "again and again returning to it [a puzzle] until it was cleared up."

Both imply their agreement rather than state it outright; Spencer by his use of the word "forthwith" and Mill by his words "again and again." Here the practice of both differs from that of the vast majority of men. Yet neither thinker seemed to be clearly conscious how it differed. The average man (that mythical creature!) when he has just been confronted with a problem, may wrestle with it with all the vigor of a great thinker. But as he sees difficulties multiplying about him, he gradually becomes more and more discouraged. Finally he throws up the problem in disgust, contenting himself with the reflection that it cannot be solved, or that it will take somebody who knows more than he to solve it.

A real thinker, however, if confronted with the same problem, will look for a solution from every possible viewpoint. But failing an answer he will not give up. Instead he will let the subject drop for a while, say a couple of weeks or perhaps longer, and then refer to it again. This time he will find that certain obscurities have become a little clearer; that certain questions have been answered. He will again attack his puzzle with energy. And if he does not obtain a complete solution he will once more put it aside, returning to it after another interval, until finally a satisfactory solution presents itself.

You may fail to see any difference between thinking for two hours separated by two weeks, and thinking for two consecutive hours. As an experiment, then, the next time you come across a puzzle which you fail to solve at first tilt, write down all the unsatisfactory solutions suggested, and all the questions, difficulties and objections met with. You may leave this for a few weeks. When you return to it a few of the difficulties will look less formidable, and some of the questions will have practically answered themselves. (Of course some of the difficulties may look more formidable, and a few new questions may have arisen.) If a solution is not found at the second attempt, the problem may again be sent to your mental waiting room. But if it is only of reasonable difficulty a solution is bound, soon or late, to be discovered.

It is difficult to say just what effects this change in thought, when apparently one has engaged in no reflection during the interval. The attempted solution probably gives a certain "set" to our minds. Without being aware of it we observe facts relating to our problem. Ideas which occur to us in other connections are unconsciously seen in their bearing on the unsolved question. In short, "those proclivities of thought which have probably been caused unawares by experience" make themselves felt.

It may be imagined that if we think too much we will be liable permanently to injure our mighty intellects. This has sometimes happened. But there is no serious danger of it. Thinking on one useful subject for a long while will not hurt you any more than thinking on a thousand different useless subjects for the same period. But of course you should not try to concentrate when you are sleepy, when you have a headache, when some other bodily pain distracts your attention, or when your mind is in any way tired. If you attempt to concentrate at these times you will endanger your mental and physical health. Not only this, but the thinking done during such periods will be of such poor quality that it will be practically useless if not harmful. This applies even to cases where mental fatigue is almost inappreciable. Thinking done in the evening seldom approaches in efficacy the thinking done in the first hours of the morning. But you should always make sure your mind is actually tired. It may merely be tired of a particular subject.

An objection of a different kind may be raised against concentrating at every opportunity. It has often been noticed that names have been recalled and problems solved when we were thinking of something else. It may be urged that such solutions would not have occurred when concentrating, because the exact associations which led up to them would not have been present. This is occasionally true. But there are still reasons why I must maintain my position. No matter how well a man may have trained himself to concentrate, there will always be short periods when his mind will wander, and these will suffice for any accidental associations. Moreover, the fact that these mind wandering periods *occasionally* do good does not excuse their existence. The most fallacious ideas, the most demoniacal practices, the most despicable characters of history, have *occasionally* done good. The fact is that for every useful association which occurs during mind wandering, ten associations just as useful will occur during concentration. The only reason useful mind wandering associations appear frequent is that they are unexpected, therefore more noticed when they come.

It has been frequently said that many of the world's greatest inventions were due to accident. In a sense this is true. But the accident was prepared for by previous hard thinking. It would never have occurred had not this thinking taken place. It is said that the idea of gravitation came to Newton because an apple fell on his head. Perhaps. But apples had been falling ever since there were apple trees, and had probably been falling on men's heads ever since men had acquired the habit of getting their heads in the way. The idea of the steam engine is supposed to have come to Watt while observing a tea kettle. But how many thousands before him had not seen steam coming out of kettles? The idea of the pendulum for regulating time occurred to Galileo from observing a swinging lantern in a cathedral. Think how many others must have seen that lantern swinging! It is probable that in all these cases the invention or idea had been prepared for, had been all but formed, by downright hard thinking in previous periods of concentration. All that was needed was the slightest unusual occurrence to make the idea complete and conscious. The unusual occurrence, the accident, which has so often received the credit for the invention or the idea, merely made it come sooner, for with the thinking these men did, it was bound to come eventually. . . .

Of course I really do not seriously expect anybody to concentrate at every opportunity. I don't myself. I merely wanted to establish the fact that it's the best thing. But every man, even the tired business variety, should set aside at least half an hour a day, or three and a half hours a week. I realize what a great hardship it is for some people to devote one-forty-eighth of their time to such a useless pastime as thinking. But if they will make the sacrifice for seven consecutive days they will find themselves bearing up nobly at the end.

There is even a possibility that they may be encouraged to extend the time.

V

PREJUDICE AND UNCERTAINTY

"FROM time to time there returns upon the cautious thinker, the conclusion that, considered simply as a question of probabilities, it is decidedly unlikely that his views upon any debatable topic are correct. 'Here,' he reflects, 'are thousands around me holding on this or that point opinions differing from mine—wholly in most cases; partially in the rest. Each is as confident as I am of the truth of his convictions. Many of them are possessed of great intelligence; and, rank myself high as I may, I must admit that some are my equals—perhaps my superiors. Yet, while every one of us is sure he is right, unquestionably most of us are wrong. Why should not I be among the mistaken? True, I cannot realize the likelihood that I am so. But this proves nothing; for though the majority of us are necessarily in error, we all labor under the inability to think we are in error. Is it not then foolish thus to trust myself? When I look back into the past, I find nations, sects, philosophers, cherishing beliefs in science, morals, politics, and religion, which we decisively reject. Yet they held them with a faith quite as strong as ours; nay—stronger, if their intolerance of dissent is any criterion. Of what little worth, therefore, seems this strength of my conviction that I am right? A like warrant has been felt by men all the world through; and, in nine cases out of ten, has proved a delusive warrant. Is it not then absurd in me to put so much faith in my judgments?' " [1]

I trust the reader will pardon this second rather extended quotation from Herbert Spencer, but the thought expressed must be kept in mind if we are to approach our present subject in the proper spirit. . . .

Our subject is prejudice. Our object is to free ourselves as much as possible from our own prejudices. But before we can get rid of a thing it is first necessary to recognize that thing when we see it.

[1] Essay, *Over-Legislation.*

Prejudice is often confused with intolerance. They are not the same. A man may be prejudiced and not intolerant. You may think that your alma mater, your city, or your country, is the greatest in the world, for little other reason than simply that it is *yours*. Your opinion is prejudiced. But you may not protest if any other man thinks that *his* alma mater, or *his* city, or *his* country, is the best in the world. In fact you may not have much respect for him if he doesn't think so. And your opinion is tolerant.

On the other hand, a man may be intolerant and not prejudiced. You may decide, solely on the evidence and on grounds of pure reason, that paper money—fiat money—is always a harmful form of currency, and you may be justly wrathful against the man who advocates it. You may even wish him suppressed. Yet you may be able to answer all his arguments. But you fear that if he is allowed to air his views they will take hold on minds as shallow as his own. You fear that once they have taken root it will be difficult to dislodge them, and that in the meanwhile they may do harm by being put into practice. You are intolerant. But you are not prejudiced. It is well to remember this distinction when accusations of prejudice are flying through the ozone.

One thing more must be kept in mind. Prejudice has less connection with truth and falsity than is generally supposed. The fact that a man is unprejudiced does not make his opinion right. And the fact that a man is prejudiced does not necessarily make his opinion wrong; though it must be admitted that if it is right it will be so only by accident.

It is often thought that prejudice can be immediately recognized. Locke says, "Every one is forward to complain of the prejudices that mislead other men or parties, as if he were free and had none of his own. . . . This is the mote which every one sees in his brother's eye, but never regards the beam in his own.'' [2] However, slight consideration will convince us that because one man accuses another of prejudice, it does not follow that the accused is guilty. The general practice is to accuse of prejudice

[2] *The Conduct of the Understanding.*

any one whose views happen to differ from our own.

Let us consider a formal dictionary definition of prejudice: "Judgment formed without due examination; opinion adverse to anything, without just grounds or sufficient knowledge." This is not altogether satisfactory. A man may form a judgment without sufficient knowledge and still be unprejudiced. He may be perfectly open minded and willing to change his opinion if other evidence is adduced. But even if the formation of a judgment without sufficient knowledge is prejudice, it is often justified. At all events, every one will agree that the foregoing definition helps us little in discovering our own prejudices. All of us, for instance, believe our judgment on any given question has been formed with due examination, each being his own judge of what constitutes "due."

It is difficult to find any satisfactory definition. Perhaps the best I can do is to point out various specific forms of prejudice and their causes. The first form of prejudice I shall name consists in a love for, and a desire to hold, some opinion. We may roughly ascribe this desire to three causes:

(1) We desire an opinion to be right because we would be personally benefited if it were. Promise a man that if he invests his money in the Lookgood Gold Mine he will receive dividends of over 40 per cent. annually, and he is in danger of becoming extremely gullible. He shirks looking up the previous record of the promoters or directors because he has a secret and indefined fear that if he does he will find their pictures in the Rogues' Gallery. Advertise in a magazine that any thin man can gain seven to fourteen pounds a week by drinking Fattilac and you will receive hundreds of answers enclosing the fifty cents for a trial bottle. Not one desperately slim man in ten will stop to ask himself how the miracle can be performed. In fact, he will do his worst to argue himself into the matter. He will tell himself that the advertisement is in a reliable magazine, that the company would not dare to make an assertion like that unless it could make good, that . . .

But we may pass over the more obvious benefits, and proceed to those causes of prejudice less consciously selfish or directly beneficial. If an economist were to write a book attempting to prove that bankers were really unnecessary and could be dispensed with, it is a rather sure guess that a banker would not regard very highly the intellectual powers of that economist. If he considered his arguments at all, it would be only with the view of refuting them. In an even less conscious way, a rich man is likely to oppose socialism or communism, not so much because he has evidence of intrinsic worth against them, but because he fears that if such systems of society were put into effect he would lose most of his wealth. The man who has nothing is likely to look with favor upon these schemes, because they offer him promise of better things.

The mere fact that we are ignorant of a certain thing will prejudice us against it, while knowledge of it will prepossess us in its favor. Ten chances to one a person who has been taught Esperanto will favor the adoption of an international language—and the adoption of

Esperanto in particular. Most of the remarks on the uselessness of the classics come from those ignorant of them; while those who, in order to get a college degree or for some like reason, have been forced to study Greek and Latin, will generally always exaggerate their importance. Most of the opposition to simplified spelling is due to the fact that having taken the time and toil to master our atrociously inconsistent spelling, people have a vague fear that if a phonetic system were adopted, children, the ignorant classes and persons of poor memories would be able to spell just as well as they, without one quarter the trouble of learning. Not that they are conscious of this childish and unworthy attitude, for usually they are not, but the motive is operative none the less.

Of course in all the foregoing cases of prejudice, as in those to follow, none of the victims ever uses any of his real reasons in argument, though he will bring forward nearly every other reason on earth to justify his belief. And to do him justice, it must be admitted that he is often unaware of the true cause of his inclination to one side rather than another.

Though it is less directly selfish, the patriotic bias may fairly be classed with the prejudices we have just been considering. At this time the most stupendous war of all history is raging. But I know of no German or Austrian or Turk or Bulgarian who has so far admitted that the British or the French or the Russians or the Italians or the Belgians or the Servians or the Montenegrins or the Japanese can by any possibility have right on their side, nor do I know of any Japanese or Montenegrin or Servian or Belgian or Italian or Russian or Frenchman or Englishman who believes that the Bulgarians or the Turks or the Austrians or the Germans are in the right. Philosophers and men of science are no exception; Münsterberg, Eucken and Haeckel write publicly in favor of Germany and fifty of England's foremost authors unanimously sign a pronunciamento in support of their native country—yet nobody is surprised.

(2) Another reason why we desire an opinion to be right is because we already happen to hold it. As one writer expresses it, "We often form our opinions on the slightest evi-

dence, yet we are inclined to cling to them with grim tenacity.'' There are two reasons for this.

When we have formed an opinion on anything, the chances are that we have communicated it to some one, and have thereby committed ourselves to that side. Now, to reverse an opinion is to confess that we were previously wrong. To reverse an opinion is to lay ourselves open to the charge of inconsistency. To be inconsistent—to admit that our judgments are human and fallible—this is the last thing we can ever think of. ''Inconsistency,'' said Emerson, ''is the hobgoblin of little minds.'' And if by this he meant inconsistency in the sense of changing opinions already formed, we must agree with him.

The hypothesis maker has a specific form of this fear of inconsistency. This type of theorist makes a supposition to account for certain facts. When he meets with certain allied facts for which the supposition apparently does not account, he either ignores said facts, or cuts and trims them, or bullies them into his theory. Hypotheses *per se* have never done any harm. In fact they are indispensable in all thought, especially as an aid to observation. But it is the desire to prove an hypothesis correct, simply because it is *our* hypothesis, or because it is a fascinating hypothesis, which has done harm. Darwin says that he had made it a habit "whenever a published fact, a new observation or thought came across me, which was opposed to my general results, to make a memorandum of it without fail and at once; for I had found by experience that such facts and thoughts were far more apt to escape from the memory than favorable ones."

The second reason for desiring to cling to an opinion because we already hold it is one which could probably best be explained by physiological psychology and a study of the brain. We feel almost a physical pain when a tenet we have long cherished is torn up and exposed. The longer we hold an opinion, the harder it is for us to get rid of it. In this respect it is similar to habit. Nor is the comparison an analogy merely. An opinion is a habit of thought. It has the same basis in the brain, and is subject to the same laws, as a habit of

action. It is well known that the opinions of a
man over forty are pretty well set. The older
a man grows, the harder it is for him to change
an opinion—or for others to change it for him.

The side of a controversy we see first is
usually the side we see last. This is because
the arguments we meet do not have to shake up
or dislodge anything in our brain (unless we
are very critical, and we generally aren't).
But once let an opinion gain entrance, and any
opinion contrary to it will have to dislodge the
old one before it can find a place for itself.

And as Mark Twain has remarked, "When
even the brightest mind in our world has been
trained from childhood in a superstition of any
kind, it will never be possible for that mind,
in its maturity, to examine sincerely, dispassionately, and conscientiously any evidence or
any circumstance which shall seem to cast a
doubt upon the validity of that superstition."
Of course Mark Twain was wrong. Of course
we are The Reasoning Race, as he cynically in-
timates we are not. To religion, for instance,
the most important question which can engage
our understanding, each of us always gives in-

dependent thought. It is a mere accident, of
course, that almost all of the 400,000,000 China-
men are Buddhists. It is a mere accident that
the overwhelming mass of East Indians are
Brahmans. It is only by chance that practically all Turks, Persians and Arabians are
Mohammedans. And it merely happened to
happen that England is Protestant and Ireland
is Catholic. . . . But it is unsafe to bring this
question of religion too near home.

We now come to our third cause of desire:

(3) We desire an opinion to be wrong because we would be forced to change other opinions if it were not; or we desire an opinion to
be right because then we would be able to retain our other opinions. This is a most wide-
spread form of prejudice. But I believe it is,
fortunately, the most defensible. Its defensi-
bility, however, depends mainly on the opinions
we fear to change. These we may divide into
two kinds:

(a) Those which have been formed without
thought; borrowed opinions, etc. The greatest
opposition to the theory of evolution came from
those conservative Christians who saw that it

undermined any literal interpretation of Genesis. If these Christians had investigated the sources of that book, had considered its probable authority, had given thought to the possibility of inspired writing, and had finally decided in favor of the Biblical narrative; then—right or not—their opposition to Darwin's theory would have been free at least from this sort of prejudice. But most of this opposition had come from persons who had not thought of Genesis, but had accepted it from the first, because it had been dogmatically hammered into their heads since childhood. Hence it was prejudice, pure and simple.

(b) The second kind of opinions we fear to change are those resting mainly upon evidence. William James gives an example:

"Why do so few 'scientists' even look at the evidence for telepathy, so-called? Because they think, as a leading biologist, now dead, once said to me, that even if such a thing were true, scientists ought to band together to keep it suppressed and concealed. It would undo the uniformity of nature, and all sorts of other things without which scientists cannot carry on their pursuits." [3] Darwin writes that when a youth he told Sedgwick the geologist of how a tropical Volute shell had been found in a gravel pit near Shrewsbury. Sedgwick replied that some one must have thrown it there, and added that if it were "really imbedded there, it would be the greatest misfortune to geology, as it would overthrow all that we know about the superficial deposits of the Midland Counties"— which belonged to the glacial period.[4]

Some readers may object to calling the last case prejudice. They may say that Sedgwick was perfectly justified. That, however, is not the present question. Prejudice itself may sometimes be justified. But Sedgwick tacitly admitted that he not only believed the shell had not been imbedded, he actually *desired* that it had not been. And our desires always determine, to a great extent, the trouble we take to get evidence, and the importance we attach to it after we have it.

Emerson's remark, that inconsistency is the hobgoblin of little minds, is true in a double sense. For not only is it harmful to fear to

[3] *The Will to Believe.*   [4] *Autobiography.*

change an opinion which we have entertained,
it is even harmful at times to fear to hold
simultaneously two opinions incongruous with
one another. If a thought springs up in your
mind, and you come to see after a time that it
is inconsistent with another thought, do not immediately try to throw out one or the other. Instead, think the new thought out in all its bearings and implications, just as if you had never
had the first. Perhaps follow the same practice
with the first idea. By and by one will reveal
its falsity and the other its truth. Or more
likely you will find that there was some truth in
each idea, and you will reconcile the two in a
truth higher, deeper, or more comprehensive.

I have set down these three cases of prejudice to help the reader in recognizing the same
or similar prejudices in himself. And the mere
recognition of prejudices as prejudices will do
much toward their elimination. But though we
all strenuously maintain our anxiety to get rid
of prejudices, the real reason most of us have
them is that we do not want to get rid of them.
We are all willing to get rid of prejudice in

the abstract. But when some one troubles himself to point out any particular concrete prejudice of ours we defend it and cling to it like a dog to his bone. The only way we can get rid of this desire to cling to our prejudices, is thoroughly to convince ourselves of the superiority of the truth; to leave not the slightest doubt in our own minds as to the value of looking with perfect indifference on all questions; to see that this is more advantageous than believing in that opinion which would benefit us most if true, more important than "being consistent," more to be cherished than the comfortable feeling of certainty. When we really do desire to get rid of our prejudices we will put ourselves on the path of getting rid of them. And not before then.

One more prejudice has yet to be considered. This may be called the prejudice of imitation. We agree with others, we adopt the same opinions of the people around us, because we fear to disagree. We fear to differ with them in thought in the same way that we fear to differ with them in dress. In fact this parallel between style in thought and style in clothing

seems to hold throughout.   Just as we fear to
look different from the people around us because we will be considered freakish, so we fear
to think differently because we know we will be
looked upon as "queer."   If we have a number
of such dissenting opinions we will be regarded
as anything from a mere crank to a fanatic or
one with a "screw loose."   When our backs are
turned people will wisely point their index fin-
gers to their temples and move them around in
little circles.

Our fear of freak opinions is only equalled
by our dread of ideas old-fashioned.   A little
while ago it was considered popular to laugh
at the suffragettes.   And everybody laughed.
Now it is getting to be popular to laugh at the
anti-suffragettes.   A little while ago it was considered quite *comme il faut* to fear socialism.
Now it is becoming proper to remark, "There is
really quite a good deal of truth in their theories."   And soon we shall doubtless all be out
and out socialists.

Nor is the prejudice of imitation confined to
the layman.   If anything, it is even more common among so-called "thinkers."   I remember

quoting some remark of Spencer to an acquaintance, and getting this: "Yes, but isn't Herbert Spencer's philosophy considered dead?" This same acquaintance also informed me that John Stuart Mill had been "superseded." He candidly admitted—in fact seemed rather proud of the fact—that he had read practically nothing of either philosopher. I am not trying to defend Spencer or John Stuart Mill, nor am I attempting to bark at the heels of any of our present-day philosophers. But I am willing to wager that most of these same people now so dithyrambic in their praise of James, Bergson, Eucken and Russell will twenty-five years hence be ashamed to mention those names, and will be devoting themselves solely to Post-neo-futurism, or whatever else happens to be the passing fadosophy of the moment.

If this is the most prevalent form of prejudice it is also the most difficult to get rid of. This requires moral courage. It requires the rarest kind of moral courage. It requires just as much courage for a man to state and defend an idea opposed to the one in fashion as it would for a city man to dress coolly on a sweltering day, or for a young society woman to attend a smart affair in one of last year's gowns. The man who possesses this moral courage is blessed beyond kings, but he must pay the fearful price of ridicule or contempt.

There is another form of this prejudice of imitation radically opposed to this. Just as with fashions in clothes there are people who strive to imitate others, so there are people who devote themselves entirely to being "different." Their greatest fear is that they will be taken for "one of the mob." They dress themselves as uniquely as possible in order to acquire "individuality." We have these same people in the realm of thought. They are in constant trepidation lest they say something that everybody else says. They say things not for the sake of truth but for humor or paradox. Their great delight is to affirm or defend something "new" regardless of its truth; something deliciously radical which will shock everybody else and startle even themselves. The worst part of this is that these people gradually come to regard their propositions as true, just as a liar finally comes to believe his own lies.

The only cure for such a mental condition is a constant sincerity in every opinion we advance. People are often led into the fault by a motive not incommendable in itself—the desire for originality. But they choose the wrong path to their goal. If you make originality and radicalness your aim, you will attain neither truth nor originality. But if you make truth your aim you will very likely get truth, and originality will come of itself.

There are hundreds of prejudices, hundreds of forms of prejudice. There is, for instance, the prejudice of conservatism, which manifests itself in a vague fear that if the present order were changed in any particular—if women were given the vote, if socialism were to triumph, if a new filing system were to be installed at the office—all would be lost. But I cannot deal adequately with all the forms of bias which flock to mind.

The distinguishing mark of the great thinkers of the ages was their comparative freedom from the prejudices of their time and community. In order to avoid these prejudices one must be constantly and uncompromisingly sounding his own opinions. Eternal vigilance is the price of an open mind.

Prejudice is not the only danger which lies in wait for the would-be thinker. In his very efforts to get rid of prejudice he is liable to fall into an even greater intellectual sin. This sin is uncertainty.

As uncertainty and doubt are nearly synonymous, the reader will probably be surprised at this statement because of the praise I have hitherto accorded to the doubtful attitude. But the doubtful attitude, necessary and praiseworthy as it is, should not be maintained always. We think in order to have opinions. We have opinions in order to guide action; in order to act upon should occasion require. Herbert Spencer, even after his remarks quoted at the beginning of this chapter, which imply the need of extreme caution, adds, ". . . In daily life we are constantly obliged to act out our inferences, trustless as they may be— . . . in the house, in the office, in the street, there hourly arise occasions on which we may not hesitate; seeing that if to act is dangerous, never to act at all is fatal. . . ."

There are other reasons why we cannot afford to keep the doubtful attitude. If our lives were interminable, if we had limitless time for thinking, we could afford to remain in doubt indefinitely. But life is fleeting. So if you have examined facts obtainable on such a question as psychic phenomena, have kept your mind open for a certain time, and have decided that communication with the dead is impossible, you are justified in discontinuing to look for evidence on that question. Every hour devoted to examining such evidence would be an hour taken away from thought on some other subject, and the law of diminishing returns is just as applicable in thinking as in economics.

Another trouble with the attitude of doubt is that when not properly utilized it hinders rather than aids the acquisition of truth. This is especially the case when it takes the form of *fear of prejudice*. If guided by this fear, in our anxiety not to discriminate in favor of one side of a question we are apt to discriminate in favor of the other. In an attempt to give an opposing argument due consideration, we are liable to give it undue consideration. Instead of removing prejudice with reason we may be trying to balance one prejudice with a counter prejudice. When a person disagrees with him, a very conscientious thinker, fearing that he may be prejudiced, and in order to prove himself broad-minded, will often say regarding an objection, "Well, there may be something in that." Now your only excuse for ever saying, "There may be something in that," will be as an attitude to assume in experimenting or observing, or looking up material or arguments to find whether there actually *is* anything in it. Then, if you do not find anything in it you are justified in saying so—and you ought to.

It is useless to stimulate doubt unless you intend, on grounds of reason, to settle the doubt. *The doubtful attitude should be maintained only so long as you are actively searching for evidence bearing on a question.* Maintained at any other time or used in any other way it means merely uncertainty, indefiniteness, vagueness, and leads nowhere.

It is important that we be unprejudiced. It is even more important that our views be definite. And if our definite views are wrong? . . . But the words of Thomas Huxley on this subject cannot be improved:

"A great lawyer-statesman and philosopher of a former age—I mean Francis Bacon—said that truth came out of error much more rapidly than it came out of confusion. There is a wonderful truth in that saying. Next to being right in this world, the best of all things is to be clearly and definitely wrong, because you will come out somewhere. If you go buzzing about between right and wrong, vibrating and fluctuating, you come out nowhere; but if you are absolutely and thoroughly and persistently wrong, you must, some of these days, have the extreme good fortune of knocking your head against a fact, and that sets you all straight again." [5]

When you find yourself fluctuating back and forth between two opinions you might find it helpful to hold an internal debate. State to yourself as strongly as possible the case for the affirmative, and then put as convincingly as pos-

[5] *Science and Education.*

sible the case for the negative, holding a refutation if necessary. You may even elaborate this by writing the arguments for both sides in parallel columns. Of course you should never use an argument which you can see on its face to be fallacious, nor a statement which represents merely a prejudice and nothing more. You should use only such arguments as you think a sincere debater would conscientiously employ. By thus making your reasons articulate you will often find that there is really no tenable case at all for one side, and you will seldom fail to reach a definite conclusion. This method of arriving at a decision may be voted childish and even artificial, but nothing is to be despised which can render intellectual help.

One word more on this. There is a type of individual, most often met with among writers, who fears to make a statement of his thought definite, because he has a faint suspicion that it may be wrong. He wishes to allow himself plenty of loopholes to slip out of an intellectual position in case any one should attack it. Hence he never says outright, "Such and such

is the case.'' Instead, his talk or writing is
guarded on all sides by such expressions as ''It
is probable that,'' ''it is possible that,'' ''the
facts *seem to* indicate that''; or ''such and such
is *perhaps* the case.'' Not satisfied with this
he makes his statement less positive by preceding it with an ''I believe,'' or worse yet, with an
''*I am inclined* to believe.''

This is often done under the impression that
it is something noble, that it signifies broadmindedness, lack of dogmatism, and modesty.
It may. If it does, so much the worse for
broadmindedness, lack of dogmatism, and modesty. Never yield to the temptation to word
your thoughts in this manner. If you truly and
firmly believe that ''such and such is the case''
say ''such and such is the case''; not ''it is possible that such and such is the case,'' or ''such
and such is perhaps the case,'' or ''it is my belief that such and such is the case.'' People
will assume that it is your belief and not somebody else's.

Suppose you have made a positive statement.
And suppose you later find it to be wrong?
Well then, acknowledge that it is wrong. Ac-

knowledge that you have done something human; that you have done something which every man before you has done; that you have made a mistake. I realize such a confession is hard. It is the severest blow you can deal to yourself, and few people will think the better of you for doing it. Most of them will say, "See, he acknowledges himself that he was wrong." And with these people, both you and your theory will be far more discredited than if you had clung to it until the end of your life, no matter how obviously, how flagrantly, it opposed itself to facts. But a few people will appreciate your sacrifice. A few people will admire your bigness. And you will grow. You will grow as a thinker. What is more, you will grow morally. And the time will come when you will have fewer and fewer occasions to reverse yourself, for you will learn to think longer before you advocate an opinion.

The question of the avoidance of prejudice and the necessity of breaking off doubt, remains still unsettled. There can be no doubt that the two desideratums conflict; that to cut off doubt, or even to refrain from stimulating it, is to encourage by so much the dominance of prejudice.

The answer to this question will depend entirely upon the particular problem under consideration. No rules can be laid down. Everything will depend upon the importance of the question, upon the possibility or frequency of occasions when we may be called to act upon the answer, and upon the way in which the answer will affect conduct when we do act upon it. Where the importance of the question is trifling, it would be foolish to sound our prejudices too deeply, or to go to any elaborate pains to collect evidence. Where immediate, unhesitating action is required, remaining in doubt might be fatal. Any decision would be better than no decision. When the importance of the question is vital, or when the possibility of having to act on the answer is distant, we can afford to preserve our doubts, to suspend final judgment, for years—perhaps during our entire life; and we should spare no pains to investigate fully all that relates to the question.

Just how much trouble to take, how long to

keep alive the attitude of doubt in any particular question, will have to be decided by the individual. His own judgment must be the sole criterion.

VI

DEBATE AND CONVERSATION

THE mind engages in many activities which have power either for evil or good. Just what influence they will exert depends on how we use them. One of the most important of these activities is debate.

Debate brings in that unequaled form of incentive for all action which psychologists call "social pressure" and which here means nothing more than the desire to excel a fellow-being in some line of endeavor. When debating we concentrate, and we do so without conscious effort. We are too interested in defeating our opponent to wander from the subject. We are forced to think rapidly. Not least of all, we are compelled to think articulately.

But with all its advantages, debate is one of the most potent sources of prejudice. In the heat of controversy, we adopt any and every argument that comes handy. Every statement of our opponent is considered only in the light of how it can be refuted. We are willing to use almost any objection against him, so long as we believe he will see no flaw in it. It is of utmost importance that we find how to avoid these pitfalls.

The first thing we must do is to adopt a complete change of attitude toward an opponent's arguments. Whenever we meet with a fact which we would not like to cite in a debate; because, to put it mildly, it would not help our side; we should carefully investigate that fact. We should consider whether if true it changes the aspect of things. We should get rid of the idea that in order to vindicate our side we must answer every contention our opponent advances. For this opponent of ours will very likely be a man in full possession of his senses; at least some of his arguments will be rational. When they are, we should be willing to acknowledge it. Their truth does not necessarily make his side right. His arguments may be irrelevant; they may be outbalanced by some other reason or reasons. At-

tempts to prove too much are liable to put us
into the position of the lawyer whose client is
alleged to have been sued for putting a hole in
a borrowed umbrella. The lawyer proved first,
that his client did not borrow the umbrella; second, that there was a hole in it when he got it;
third, that there was nothing the matter with it
when he returned it.

After you have had a friendly argument with
an acquaintance, you take leave either with the
satisfaction that you have bested him, or with
a vague consciousness that though you were
right, he was just a trifle more skillful at bring-
ing forward arguments. But having this satisfaction or dissatisfaction, you seldom think any
more of the matter until the next time you meet
him. Now this practice is helpful neither to
your debating nor your thinking. After you
have taken leave of your acquaintance, and are
left to the quietude of your own thoughts, you
should mentally run over your controversy.
You should dispassionately consider the bearing
and weight of his arguments; and then, reviewing your own, ask yourself which were valid
and relevant and which were not. If you find

you have used a sophism you should resolve
never to use it again, even though your opponent may have been unable to answer it. The
question of morals aside, this is poor practice if
you ever hope to become a thinker. In the end,
it will tell against you even as a debater.

You can use your debates for constructive material as well as for criticism. After a controversy you can go over the arguments of your
opponent which you could not refute, or refuted
but lamely, and think of the answers you might
have given. Of course you should take care
that these answers are not sophistical. The
question will very likely come up again; if not
with the same friend, then with another, and
when it does you will find yourself prepared.

But the best debater, or at least he who gets
the most from debating, is the man who looks
for evidence and thinks not for debate, but to
obtain a correct conclusion. After he has
reached a conclusion in this manner, he does not
advance every possible reason to support it.
He does not even utilize the reasons on which
others base a similar belief, if he does not himself accept these reasons. He states merely

that evidence and those reasons which have led him to accept his conclusion, nothing more.

While we are considering debate, I may well say a few words about conversation in general. We do not and cannot always argue with our friends, even though we scorn the dictums of formal etiquette. But because we do not argue, it does not follow that we gain nothing. In fact, ordinary conversation has advantages numerous over debate, not the least of which is the comparative freedom it gives from prejudice. But the value of conversation depends both on what we talk about, and whom we talk with. Too much of our talk is on petty matters, is uneducative. And even if we converse on worthy topics, it will profit us little if we do not talk with worthy people. When we commune with a dull mind, our thoughts are forced, in some degree, down to the level of that mind. But dull people do not usually talk of weighty matters, nor do active intellects dwell long on trifles. Therefore if we rightly choose our companion we can conscientiously leave our path of conversation to choose itself.

One aspect of conversation remains to be

treated—its corrective power. "There is a sort of mental exposure in talking to a companion; we drag our thoughts out of their hiding-places, naked as it were, and occasionally we are not a little startled at the exhibition. Unexpressed ideas are often carefully cherished until, placed before other eyes as well as our own, we see them as they really are."[1]

[1] T. Sharper Knowlson, *The Art of Thinking*.

VII

THINKING AND READING

UP to now I have dealt with thinking almost as if it could be carried on without external aid. As with cautionary and constructive thought, I have perhaps been led to do this because of a reaction from the usual insistence upon reading as indispensable to mental improvement, and the corresponding neglect of the need for independent thinking. Men thought before there were books, and men can still think without reading, but they cannot . . . I was about to remark that they could not read without thinking, but on second thought I am inclined to doubt it. However, we have clung to the natural order, for we first considered unaided thinking, then the help given by conversation and dispute, and finally we are to examine the aid rendered by reading. There can be no doubt that this order follows the de-

velopment of thought both in the individual and
in the human race.

While no complaint can be made of lack of
quantity in what has been written on reading,
most of it has not taken up the subject from
the proper standpoint; still less has dealt with
it in the right manner. There has been counsel galore urging people to read; and recently
there has been a great deal of advice on what to
read. But comparatively very little has been
said on *how* to read. At one time reading was
regarded an untainted virtue, later it was seen
that it did us no good unless we read good books,
and now there is a dawning consciousness that
even if we read good books they will benefit us
little unless we read them in the right way.

But even where this consciousness has been
felt, little attempt has been made to solve the
problem systematically. Leisurely discourses,
pretty aphorisms, and dogmatic rules have been
the forms in which the question has been dealt
with. Such conflicting adages as "A good book
should be read over and over again"; and "The
art of reading is the art of skipping," are not

very serviceable. The necessity of some sort of orderly treatment is evident.

Before we consider how to read, some queer person may ask us to put the previous question, "Should we read at all?" Now the value of reading has, in times past, been seriously doubted by thinkers and non-thinkers. The philosopher Democritus put out his eyes so that, ceasing to read, he might think. We are not going to follow his example. But we can readily sympathize with him when we think of the many learned men who have read themselves into dreamy stupidity; men who know what everybody else thought, but who never have any thoughts of their own. We must admit that the arguments of these cranks are at least good medicine for the prevalent belief that the more a man reads the more he will know and the better thinker he will become.

Learning to think by reading is like learning to draw by tracing. In each case we make the work of another man our basis, instead of observing directly from Nature. The practice has its value, it is true; but no man ever became a great artist by tracing, and no man will ever become a great thinker by reading. It can never become a substitute for thought. At best, as John Locke says, "Reading furnishes the mind only with materials of knowledge, it is thinking makes what we read ours." [1]

Our problem may be divided in two parts: (1) What ratio should our reading bear to independent thinking, and (2) how should we read when we do read?

It may be thought that we can learn something about the first question by investigating the practice of great thinkers. But the outcome of such an investigation is likely to be disappointment. Kant, for instance, was an omnivorous reader; so were Huxley and Sir William Hamilton; and outside the circle of philosophers, men as unlike as Gibbon, Macaulay, Milton and Thomas A. Edison. On the other hand, Spencer seldom ever read, and Hobbes is famous for his remark that if he had read as much as other men he would have known as little. Auguste Comte was unique in that he read copiously until he conceived his Positive

[1] *The Conduct of the Understanding.*

Philosophy, and then hardly at all until the end of his life.

Even were it found that most great thinkers adhered to nearly the same practice, it would prove little; for how could we tell whether they were good thinkers on account of, or in spite of it?

We can agree a priori, however, with the remark of Schopenhauer that "the safest way to have no thoughts of one's own is to take up a book every moment one has nothing else to do." And we may agree with him further: "A man should read only when his thoughts stagnate at their source, which will happen often enough even with the best of minds. On the other hand, to take up a book for the purpose of scaring away one's own original thoughts is a sin against the Holy Spirit. It is like running away from Nature to look at a museum of dried plants, or gaze at a landscape in copperplate." [2]

It would be folly to lay down any fixed mathematical ratio between the time we should devote to reading and the time we should give

[2] *On Thinking for Oneself.*

to thinking. But one hour given to reading plus one hour given to. thinking would be certainly more beneficial than two hours devoted entirely to reading.

You can find quite a number of serious-minded men who put by a certain period each day for reading. But how many of them put by any time at all for thinking? It would be unjust to say they do not think. But at best their thinking is merely accidental—and apparently considered so. Surely it is as important that we lay aside a definite period each day for thinking as it is that we lay aside some time for reading. But how much this time should be and whether it should bear any specific ratio to the time given to reading can best be decided after a consideration of the problem of how to read.

This problem has unfortunately been much misconceived. Those who have laid stress on the maxim, "A good book should be read over and over again," have done so in the belief that this is the best way to get the most out of a particular book. But the object of reading is not to get the best out of any one book, but out of reading in general. A realization of this end will change our problem somewhat.

It will bring us to a consideration, for example, of the law of diminishing returns. While the more we re-read a book the more we get out of it, it must be remembered that with a few possible exceptions, every time we re-read it we add less to our knowledge than we did the previous time. This means that we can usually make much faster progress by reading other books, in which case we do not merely read over what we already know for the most part. Whether re-reading is ever justified, and when, is a question which will be considered a little later.

The law of diminishing returns applies to an entire subject as well as to a single book. That is to say, past a certain point, every book we read on a particular subject, while it will probably add to our knowledge, will not yield as much return as a book of equal merit on another subject, new to us.

The problem of reading asks how we can acquire the greatest number of ideas, and how we can arrive at truth rather than the verdict of an author. It assumes a limited time and asks how we can use that time most profitably. Not least of all, it asks how we can best combine our reading with original thought.

From the remarks already made, it is evident that we cannot prescribe any one method for dealing with all books. Even works of similar nature and merit will be treated in different ways, depending on the order in which we read them, and like conditions. The mastery of any book will not be an end in itself. It will be subordinated to the larger end of obtaining the best from reading as a whole. But for the sake of clearness, I shall for the present consider our end as the mastery of some particular subject, and shall indicate a plan of reading to best serve that end. Needful qualifications will come later.

I shall first outline a typical plan of study, and then review and explain it in detail.

Assuming you have chosen a subject, your first step should be to do a little unaided thinking on it. Next I would advise the selection of a comprehensive text book. This should be read critically and written note made of the problems taken up which you do not believe have been adequately treated, or the solutions of which are in any way unsatisfactory. These you should think out for yourself. A second book may in some cases be read in the same thorough manner as this first one, and the problems recorded in the same way. After that all books on that subject may be read "hop, skip and jump" fashion, for the new problems or solutions they suggest.

I do not expect the foregoing plan to be strictly adhered to, for the nature of the subject studied will make certain changes necessary. However, it demands more detailed explanation and perhaps defense.

Let us take up the first step advised—giving a little unaided thought to the subject. My only reason for advising "a little" thinking, is that I know if I asked more the reader would probably do nothing at all. Indeed many readers will fail to see the necessity of thinking about a subject before studying it. Many may even question the possibility of doing so. "How is a man to think about a subject on which he knows nothing?" you ask. Let us, however, consider.

The very fact that you want to study a subject implys that the phenomena with which it deals are not clear to you. You desire to study economics, for instance, because you feel that you do not understand everything you should about the production, distribution and consumption of wealth. In other words, something about these phenomena puzzles you—you have some unsolved problems. Very well. These problems are your materials. Try to solve them.

"But how can I solve them when I know nothing of economics?"

Kindly consider what a science is. A science is nothing more than the organized solution of a number of related problems. These problems and their answers have been changed and added to the ages through. But when the science first started there was no literature on it. It originated from the attempts of men to solve those problems which spontaneously occurred to them. Before they started thinking these men knew nothing of the science. The men who came after them availed themselves of the thoughts of those before, and added to these. The whole process has been one of thought added to thought. Yet, in spite of this, people still cling to the belief, even if they do not openly avow it, that we never can make any headway by thinking, but that in order to be educated, or cultured, or to have any knowledge, we must be reading, reading, reading.[3]

I almost blush for this elaborate defense. Everybody will admit the necessity for thinking —in the abstract. But how do we regard it in the concrete? When we see a man reading a good book, we think of him as educating himself. When we perceive a man without a book, even though we may happen to know that he is engaged in reflection, we do not look upon him as educating himself, though we may regard him as intelligent. In short, our habitual idea of thought is that it is a process of reviewing what we already know, but not of adding anything to our knowledge. Of course no one would openly

[3] This may seem unjustified. Witness, however, this remarkable statement in a prospectus of Charles Eliot's "Five Foot Shelf": " . . . The man who has not read the 'Wealth of Nations' is hardly qualified to speak or even think wisely on these vital subjects." If this be true, Adam Smith himself was hardly qualified because he certainly could not have read his own book before he had written it!

avow this opinion, but it is the common acting belief none the less. The objections to thought are inarticulate and half-conscious. I am trying to make them articulate in order to answer them.

To return, then, to the remark that we should use as materials for unaided thinking the problems which occur spontaneously. You will find when you begin to solve these that other problems will arise, and that up to a certain point, the deeper you go into a subject—the more critical you are in your thinking—the more problems will occur. Perhaps it would be too much to ask you to solve all of these. Yet even a little of this preliminary thinking will be of immense help in reading. It will give you a far better sense of the importance of different problems which a book considers, and you will not judge their significance merely by the space it devotes to them. An author may indeed bring before us certain problems which had not hitherto occurred, and stimulate in us a sense of their importance. But this artificial stimulation can never take the place of natural and spontaneous wonder. Once we have obtained a solution of a problem which has arisen spontaneously and from within, we do not easily forget it.   Our independent thinking, too, will have given us an idea of the difficulties presented by problems, and will make us more critical in reading and more appreciative of the solutions of an author.   Not least of all, if we read first we are extremely liable to fall into the routine and traditional ways of considering a subject, whereas if we first think, we are more likely in our insophistication to hit upon an idea of real originality.

One last objection to thinking before reading remains.   Schopenhauer has answered it in his forcible manner:

"A man may have discovered some portion of truth or wisdom after spending a great deal of time and trouble in thinking it over for himself, adding thought to thought; and it may sometimes happen that he could have found it all ready to hand in a book and spared himself the trouble.   But even so it is a hundred times more valuable, for he has acquired it by thinking it out for himself.   For it is only when we gain our knowledge in this way that it enters as an integral part, a living member, into the whole system of our thought; that it stands in complete and firm relation with what we know, that it is understood with all that underlies it and follows from it, that it wears the color, the precise shade, the distinguishing mark, of our own way of thinking, that it comes exactly at the right time, just as we felt the need for it; that it stands fast and cannot be forgotten." [4]

Despite the strong case that Schopenhauer makes out, I am satisfied with my former advice —that a little thinking will suffice. Not only because, as already said, the reader will probably do nothing if advised to do more; but because after a certain amount of thinking has been done, it is more profitable to avail ourselves of the wisdom of the ages, stored in books, and to do our thinking after we have acquired the main outlines of this wisdom. For when we think a problem out, with the feeling that even after we have obtained a solution we shall probably find it in a book later, we have not the incentive that we have when we feel we have covered most of

[4] Essay *On Thinking for Oneself.*

the old ground and that thinking may bring us into new territory.

The practice of Gibbon remains to be considered: "After glancing my eye over the design and order of a new book, I suspended the perusal until I had finished the task of self-examination; till I had revolved in a solitary walk all that I knew or believed, or had thought on the subject of the whole work, or of some particular chapter. I was then qualified to discern how much the author added to my original stock, and I was sometimes satisfied by the agreement, sometimes armed by the opposition of our ideas."[5]

The trouble with this method is that it is not critical enough; that is, critical in the proper sense. It almost amounts to making sure what your prejudices are, and then taking care to use them as spectacles through which to read. We always do judge a book more or less by our previous prejudices and opinions. We cannot help it. But our justification lies in the manner we have obtained these opinions; whether we have

[5] *Autobiography.*

infected them from our environment, or have held them because we wanted them to be true, or have arrived at them from substantial evidence and sound reasoning. If Gibbon had taken a critical attitude toward his former knowledge and opinions to make sure they were correct, and had then applied them to his reading, his course would have been more justifiable and profitable.

In certain subjects, however, Gibbon's is the only method which can with profit be used. In the study of geography, grammar, a foreign language, or the facts of history, it is well, before reading, simply to review what we already know. Here we cannot be critical because there is really nothing to reason about. Whether George Washington ought to have crossed the Delaware, whether "shall" and "will" ought to be used as they are in English, whether the verb "avoir" ought to be parsed as it is, or whether Hoboken ought to be in New Jersey, are questions which might reasonably be asked, but which would be needless, because for the purposes we would most likely have in mind in reading such facts it would be sufficient to know that these things are so. We might include mathematics among the subjects to be treated in this fashion. Though it is a rational science, there is such unanimity regarding its propositions that the critical attitude is almost a waste of mental energy. In mathematics, to understand is to agree.

We come to the second step outlined in our plan of study—the selection of a comprehensive text book.

Every large subject has gathered about it a vast literature, more than one man can ever hope to cover completely. This literature may be said to consist wholly of two things: information as to facts, and opinions on those facts. In other words, any book you read on that subject will probably contain some facts new to you and will contain also the thoughts and reflections of the author. Of course you should endeavor to learn as many facts as possible. But it is not necessary to know all that has been thought about the subject. You are supposed to have a mind of your own; you are supposed to do some thinking for yourself. But though it is not necessary that you know all that has been thought, it is well that you know at least part of what has been thought, and so far as possible, the best part. For as just pointed out, if you attempt to think out an entire subject for yourself you will expend great energy and time in arriving at conclusions which have probably already been arrived at during the generations that the subject has had its being. Therefore you should endeavor to get, in as short a time as possible, the greatest number of important facts and the main outlines of the best that has been thought.

So if you sincerely intend to master any subject, the best way to begin is by the selection of the most comprehensive and authoritative work you can secure.

The man who desires to study any subject is commonly advised to read first a small "introductory" book, then a larger one, and finally the largest and most authoritative volumes. The trouble with this practice is that you will have to study each book in turn. If you take up the most thorough book first you need merely glance through the smaller books, for the chances are that they will contain little that is new to you, unless they happen to be more recent. The only justification for reading a small book first is that the larger books are apt to be technical and to assume a certain knowledge of the subject. However, *the* authoritative treatise or treatises on a subject usually refer far less to the smaller books than the smaller books do to them. Any greater depth of thought which the larger works may possess can be made up for by increased concentration on the part of the reader. Of course if a man does not intend to master a subject thoroughly, but only to get some idea of its broad outlines, the case is different. He would then be justified in reading a small work.

Another advantage of beginning a subject with the study of a comprehensive and authoritative volume or main textbook, is that you avoid confusion. The man who has mastered one foreign language, say French, will always find his knowledge of great benefit to him for the study of another language, such as Spanish. But any one who has begun at about the same time the study of two or more foreign languages must remember his confusion, and how his vague knowledge of one tongue hindered him in the acquisition of the other.

So with reading. When we peruse a book in the usual casual way we do not master it. And when we read a book on the same subject immediately after it, the different viewpoint is liable to cause bewilderment and make us worse off than before the second book was started. We do not like to devote a lot of time to one book, but would rather run through several books in the same time, believing that we thereby gain more ideas. We are just as mistaken as a beginner in swimming who would attempt to learn several strokes before having mastered one well enough to keep afloat.

A main text being of such importance, its choice involves responsibility. But how are we to know whether one book is superior to another until we have read both? And if we are confronted with this difficulty even when familiar with a subject, how much greater must be our task when we know nothing of it? These difficulties do not appear so formidable in practice.

Failing other means, the best method of selecting a main text is by reputation. If we do not even know what book has the best reputation, we can easily find out by referring to so acknowledged an authority as the Encyclopedia Brittanica, and consulting the bibliography in the article on the subject.

But reputation does not furnish the only means of selecting. By merely glancing through a book, stopping here and there to read entire paragraphs—a task of ten or fifteen minutes—we can form an estimate which later reading will usually justify. For an author betrays himself in every line he writes; every slightest remark reveals in some manner the breadth and depth of his thought. But just how well we can judge a book in this way depends both on our own ability and on the time we devote to glancing through it.

A few general requirements in a main text have been implied in stating the purpose of having one. The book with the best reputation is not necessarily the best for you. In economics Adam Smith's *Wealth of Nations*, though easily the most famous book on the subject, would hardly be suitable as a main text because it has been superseded. But though recency is always an asset, this does not mean that the most recent book is always or even usually the best. The common idea, though it is usually but vaguely formulated, is that the writer of the more recent book has had all the previous books to draw upon, and has therefore been able to extract the best from all of them and add to this his own thoughts. The fallacy of this has been pointed out in the trenchant language of Schopenhauer:

"The writer of the new book often does not understand the old books thoroughly, and yet he is unwilling to take their exact words; so he bungles them and says in his own bad way that which has been said very much better and more clearly by the old writers, who wrote from their own lively knowledge of the subject. The new writer frequently omits the best things they say, their most striking illustrations, their happiest remarks, because he does not see their value or feel how pregnant they are. The only thing that appeals to him is what is shallow and insipid."

The value of recency will depend on the subject; while it would be essential in aviation, its importance would be far less in ethics.

It is not well to take as your main text a book presenting a number of different and conflicting viewpoints. One purpose of a main text is to avoid confusion. Do not start the study of psychology, for instance, by reading a history of the subject giving the views of different thinkers. Begin by taking up one definite system.

Finally, be sure to select a book covering the entire field. Do not, for instance, take a volume on the tariff to begin the study of economics.

We pass now to the third step advised—to read critically. By this I do not mean that we should read skeptically or to confute everything an author says. I mean simply that we should resist our natural tendency to have our minds swayed by every opinion he expresses. I mean that before allowing an idea to slip into our minds we should first challenge its truth; we should examine its evidence.

Perhaps you have listened to a debate. After the affirmative had made his impassioned plea you were all for the affirmative. When the negative came forward and presented his case, you found yourself favoring *him*. . . . Why do debaters always try to get the last say? Why is it that in a formal debate, the affirmative, which usually has the last say, is most often the side that wins? I could state the reason bluntly. But if I did the honorable judges of such controversies would not feel that their critical powers had been complimented.

The tendency to absorb the opinions of others manifests itself to just as great a degree in reading. I have held debating up as an example merely because it brings out more strongly, more strikingly, the effects of such a tendency. But how can it be resisted?

If we have thought out a subject thoroughly, if we have acquired a stock of clear and definite ideas on it, criticism in reading will largely take care of itself. By dint of our own thinking we will know what is relevant and what is not; we shall be able to judge the truth and importance of the various arguments offered. The chances are, however, that we shall not have given much previous thinking to the subject, and that even if we have we shall not have gone as far as the author, who doubtless availed himself of other books. Consequently certain problems which he takes up will not even have occurred to us, and hence will not have received our consideration.

But where our thinking has not helped us, and even where it has, we should look critically upon every statement of an author, instead of lazily acquiescing in it. The difference between critical and ordinary reading, is that in the former we look for objections, in the latter we wait until they happen to occur to us. Even then we do not hold our objections steadily in mind; we are as likely as not to accept later arguments based upon one we have previously objected to. In order to avoid this perhaps the best we can do when we object to any statement or believe we have found a fallacy, is to make written note of it in the margin. To some extent this will prevent forgetting it. Too few or too many marginal notes are both extremes to be shunned. If we make too many we shall be apt to lose a true sense of proportion and fail to distinguish essential criticisms from nonessentials. The only way we can keep clear of this extreme is to avoid quibbling and hair-splitting, making only such written criticisms as we feel we could un-

blushingly defend before the author himself.
Often however we may feel that a statement is
untrue, or that an argument is fallacious, and
yet be unable to point out just where or how it
is so.   In this case perhaps the best plan would
be merely to put a question mark in the margin
in order to remind ourselves that the statement
has not been fully accepted.

We ought to make sure what we object to because it is a peculiarity of the human mind that
it does not require evidence for a statement before accepting it; it generally accepts any statement which has no evidence against it.   Unless
we reject a statement and know why we have
done so, it is liable to insinuate itself in our reasoning, and the longer it remains the more difficult it is to get rid of it.   This is why it is so
important to avoid as many pitfalls as possible
at the beginning of a subject.

The reader may find that even when he reads
critically he will accept a certain statement at
the time; and then perhaps much later, say a
month, an objection to that statement will occur
to him, or he will see that it at least ought to
be qualified.   For an explanation of this we

must go back to an analysis of the thinking process. Every idea which enters the mind, either from independent thinking or from reading, is accepted as true if it is in full conformity with our past experience *as we remember it*. In all thinking or reading, the new idea arouses associates on its entrance. An hypothesis or principle, for instance, arouses in our minds past experiences of particular instances. If all these conform it is accepted. But in ordinary uncritical reading or thinking, only a few associates are aroused. In critical reading, we look for as many associates as possible, especially those which do not conform. It is this purpose kept in mind which helps to recall and awaken these associates. No matter how critical our attitude, however, we cannot at any given time recall every relevant associate, though later a "non-conforming" associate is likely to occur to us by pure accident.

While you are criticising a book line by line, and after you have finished reading it, you should note the importance and relevancy of the arguments accepted and rejected. While an author may make a statement with which you disagree, its truth or falsehood may not affect the rest of what he has to say, or it may affect merely a few corollaries drawn from it. In other cases the truth of his entire conclusion may depend upon it. Again, an author may incontrovertibly prove something—which is entirely without bearing on the subject. This means that you should keep the precise question constantly before your mind.

Often you will find an author making a statement which really amounts to nothing more than a mere airing of his prejudices, or at best the bare statement of a conclusion. If he says, "Socialism is the greatest menace of our civilization," and leaves it go at that, not telling how or why, you should mentally note this as a statement, as a statement merely; you should not allow it to influence your opinion either way. Finally, remember that though you may be able to refute every argument an author brings forward in support of a conclusion, his conclusion may still be correct. It is possible for a man to be right for the wrong reasons.

While I believe all the foregoing suggestions are judicious and necessary, I am willing to admit that their wisdom may reasonably be doubted. But there is one practice about which there can be no controversy—that of making sure you thoroughly understand every idea of an author. While most people will not verbally contradict this advice, their actual practice may be a continual contradiction of it. They will be in such haste to finish a book that they will not stop to make sure they really understand the more difficult or obscure passages. Just what they hope to gain it is difficult to say. If they think it is wasting time to try to understand every idea, it is surely a greater waste of time to read an idea without understanding it. To be sure, the difficulty of understanding may be the fault of the author. It may be due to his involved and muddled way of expressing himself. It may be the vagueness of the idea itself. But if anything this is all the greater reason why you should attempt to understand it. It is the only way you can find whether or not the author himself really knew what he was talking about. To understand thoroughly the thought of another does not necessarily mean to sympathize with it; it does not mean to ask how that

other came by it. It means merely to substitute
as far as possible concrete mental images for
the words he uses, and analyze those images to
discover to what extent they agree with facts.

Better to carry this out, you might follow another practice of immense value. Whenever
you are puzzled as to an author's meaning, or
whenever you do not care to accept his solution
of a problem but are undecided as to what the
solution is, or whenever you want to carry an
idea further than he has, or above all, whenever
an original and important relevant thought is
suggested to you, you should take your eyes
from your book—shut it if necessary—and let
your thinking flow on; give it fair play, even if
it takes an hour before your vein of suggested
thought exhausts itself. Of course this practice will prevent you from finishing a book as
soon as you otherwise would. And if finishing
a book be your aim, I have nothing to say. But
if your end is to attain true, sound knowledge,
knowledge which you will retain; if your object
is to become a thinker, the practice will prove of
unspeakable benefit. It will not interfere with
concentration. Remember your object is to con-

centrate primarily on the subject, not on the book; you intend to become a thinker, not an interpreter or a commentator or a disciple of any author.

And there are two reasons why this thinking should not be put off until after you have finished a book. The first and more important is that after you have finished reading, most of the ideas will have unrecallably dropped out of mind. The second is that when you are undecided about the solution of a problem, you will often find later arguments depending upon that solution. Unless its truth or falsity is decided in your own mind you will not know how to deal with these later arguments.

I have spoken of feeling that an argument is fallacious, and of being unable to point out just where it is so. To cease reading for a while, and to endeavor to make these inarticulate objections articulate, is excellent practice for training analytic powers and developing clearness of thought.

Another way of reading a book is what I may call the anticipating method. Whenever a writer has started to explain something, or whenever you see that he is about to, stop reading and try to think out the explanation for yourself. Sometimes such thinking will anticipate only a paragraph, at other times an entire chapter. School and college text-books, and in fact formal text-books generally, often contain lists of questions at the end of the chapters. Where you find these, read them before you read the chapter, and where possible try to answer them by your own thinking. This practice will make you understand an explanation much more easily. If your thinking agrees with the author's explanation it will give you self-confidence. It will make you realize whether or not you understand an explanation. If you were not able to think the thing out for yourself you will appreciate the author's explanation. If your thinking disagrees with that of the author you will have an opportunity to correct him— or be corrected. In either case your opinion will rest on firmer grounds. Not least of all you will be getting practice in self-thinking.

After reading and criticising a book, it is a good practice to study one taking a different viewpoint, or written even in direct opposition.

You will doubtless find that it points out many fallacies and controverts many statements in the first book, which you allowed to pass unchallenged. Ask yourself what the trouble was. Was your attitude too receptive? Did you swallow words without substituting clear mental images? Did you fail to trace out the consequences of a statement? All these questions will help you do better the next time.

Because of your ignorance of the facts, your failure to refute a conclusion will sometimes not be your fault. But even here, though you cannot contradict an author's statement of facts, you can criticise conclusions drawn from those facts.

Take an instance. In making an inquiry into the causes of fatigue, Professor Mosso of Turin selected two dogs as nearly alike as possible. One he kept tied, and the other he exercised until it was thoroughly tired. He then transfused blood of the tired dog into the veins of the rested one, and produced in the latter every sign of fatigue. From this he concluded that fatigue was due to certain poisons in the blood.

Now we cannot contradict the fact of this experiment: that the rested animal was made to look tired. But we can question the inference drawn. The truth of the conclusion aside, was the evidence sufficient to establish it? Might not, for instance, similar results have been produced upon the rested dog if blood of another rested dog had been transfused into it? Had Mosso made such an experiment? Other objections should easily occur to one.

Questions which admit of treatment by studying both sides are too numerous to mention. The literature of philosophy furnishes particularly good material. Examples which at present occur to me are Sir William Hamilton's philosophy versus Mill's *Examination of Sir William Hamilton's Philosophy,* and Herbert Spencer's *First Principles* versus William James' essay, *Herbert Spencer's Autobiography* and Henri Bergson's criticism of Spencer in his *Creative Evolution.*

Uncritical students of the history of philosophy often find themselves agreeing with each thinker in turn, no matter how much he contradicts previous thinkers, and end by acquiescing in the last system they read about. I remember

a philosophy class which completed its studies
with Pragmatism. Of course it was merely a
coincidence, but at the end of the course fully
nine-tenths of the students declared themselves
Pragmatists!

It is almost needless to remark that an author
who pretends to point out fallacies in another is
not necessarily right.   There are men who pride
themselves on "reading both sides of a subject"; but unless they have been critical, their
knowledge is not half as clear or as likely to be
true as that of a man who has read only one
side, but who has read it critically.

We have now to consider the next step outlined in the suggested plan of reading—"written note should be made of the problems taken
up which you do not believe have been adequately treated, or the solutions of which are in
any way unsatisfactory. These you should
think out for yourself."

When reading a book you will often come
across a statement, perhaps an entire chapter,
with which you disagree. This disagreement
should be recorded in the form of a question;

as for instance, "Is such and such the case?" You may doubt whether an author's explanation really explains. You may have a vague inarticulate suspicion that he is sliding over facts, or that his solution is too superficial. This suspicion should also be recorded in the form of a question. Often again, while reading, a problem connected with the subject will occur to you which the author has not even considered. This too should be recorded,

All these questions should unfailingly be written, either in the margin or on a piece of paper or notebook kept always at hand. You should then set aside a definite time for thinking and attempt to solve the questions for yourself.

And in thinking for yourself you should not make the author's remarks the basis of your thinking. You should deal with a problem almost as if it had never occurred to any one else but you. Simply because somebody else has been satisfied with a certain solution, that is no reason why you should be. You should deal directly with the facts, data and phenomena under consideration; not with the opinions of

others about those facts, data and phenomena.
You should not ask yourself whether the pragmatists are right, or whether the nominalists
are right, or the socialists, or the evolutionists,
or the Democrats, or the Presbyterians, or the
hedonists, or what not. You should not ask
yourself which "school" of thinking you ought
to belong to. You should think a problem out
for yourself, in every way that phrase implies.
At the end you may, incidentally, find yourself
agreeing in the main with some school of
thought. However, this will be only accidental,
and your thought will be much more likely to be
true. But you should never agree with a school
of thought any more than independent thinking
leads you to.

Of problems dealt with in this manner, some
will take ten minutes, others a week. If you
encounter a particularly obstinate problem it
may be best to leave it for a while, say a week
or two or even longer, and go on with other
problems. When problems are thus recurrently
treated it may take months, even years, before
a satisfactory solution is reached. In such
cases you should be willing to give months and

even years to their solution. If a problem is not important enough to devote so much time to you may be forced to abandon it; but you should constantly keep in mind the fact that you have not solved it, and you should be willing to admit to others that you have not solved it. Never allow mere intellectual laziness to stifle your doubts and make you think you have solved a problem, when you know in your heart of hearts that you have worked yourself into the state of belief merely to save yourself mental discomfort.

When most of your problems have been solved and your views made definite you may resume your reading. You may proceed to other books on the subject.

As to the suggestion that another book on the subject might be dealt with in the same manner as this first one: this will depend largely on the individual subject. It will depend on just what books have been written on that subject. If none completely or adequately covers the field, or if there are two or more good books representing radically different viewpoints, more than one book probably ought to be studied in this comprehensive manner. But this must be left to the reader's discretion.

We come now to the last part of our plan—"after that all books may be read 'hop, skip and jump' fashion, for the new problems or solutions they suggest."

I have already implied the necessity for this in formulating the law of diminishing returns. After we have read several books on a subject it would be manifestly foolish to continue reading books on that same subject *in toto*. We would merely be going over again knowledge already in our possession, instead of using our time more profitably by entering new territory. But any good book will contain *something* unique; some facts or principles to be found nowhere else; or perhaps merely an unusually clear way of explaining some old principle, or a new light on it. This we should endeavor to get without wasting our time by plowing through the entire volume.

Theoretically our problem is difficult; on its face it would seem impossible. We are to read all the important parts of a book; that is, the parts most important *for us,* and nothing but the important parts. But until we read it how are we to know whether any given part of a book is important? In practice, however, our difficulty is not so formidable.

We can eliminate the greater mass of the relatively useless part of a book by a glance at its table of contents. If we see there titles which suggest subjects or aspects of subjects in which we are not interested, or that we feel we already know enough about, or that are simply outside the particular purpose we have in consulting that book at all, we can omit those chapters and confine ourselves to the others. . . .

When we were children first learning to read we had to look at every letter in a word, then spell it out. Finally its meaning dawned upon us. As we became more proficient we did not have to look at every letter; we could read words as wholes with the same rapidity as the separate letters. Accurate psychological tests have determined that a man can read such words as "and" and "the" with even greater rapidity than any single letter composing them. We finally reach the point where we can read short phrases at the same rate as we formerly could single words.

But the secret of the scholar who can cover efficiently much more ground than ordinary men is not so much that he reads *faster,* as that he reads *less.* In other words, instead of reading every word he glances down a page and sees certain "cue" words or rather "cue" phrases, for the eye and mind take in phrases as wholes. If he is familiar with the subject (and he is not to employ this method unless and until he is) he knows immediately, by "a sort of instinct" as Buckle called it, whether any new or valuable thought is on that page. When he finds that there is he involuntarily slackens his pace and reads that thought at ordinary reading pace or even slower. Sometimes indeed he will read whole chapters slowly, word for word, if the contents are sufficiently novel and important to warrant it.

Read by this "hop, skip and jump" fashion a book the size of the present volume might take an hour or even less. But it is almost impossible to give even an approximate estimate of the time such reading ought to take. Of course the longer you spend the more you will get out of a book, but the return per time invested will be less and less. On the other hand if you read the book too fast you may be wasting your time altogether; you may end by understanding nothing at all. Much will depend upon the originality and depth of the book, upon the reader's familiarity with the subject, and upon his native mental qualities.

Many may object to practicing the foregoing method because they have a vague feeling that it is their duty to read every word in a book. I suspect that the real reason for this is simply so that when asked they can conscientiously say they have *read* the book. Whereas if they had followed this skipping method they would be able to say only that they had "glanced through it" or at best that they had "read parts of it." To this objection I have nothing to say, for I am confining my remarks to those in search of truth and knowledge rather than conversation and the good opinion of those who believe that reading from cover to cover is the only path to wisdom. I might point out in passing, however, that if we do follow this method there will be a half dozen books which we can say we have "glanced through" to one which we would otherwise have been able to say we had "read."

This way of dealing with a book is constructive and positive as opposed to the negative method of critical reading. For we read for suggestion only; we carry forward some line of thought of an author, which is better for intellectual development than trying to find if he was wrong and where he was wrong. Not only is this positive method more interesting; in some respects it is better even for criticism. For in carrying forward an author's line of thought, noting its consequences and implications and considering different cases where it applies, we find whether or not it leads to absurd conclusions; whether or not all concrete instances conform with it. It should be kept in mind that this method is not to be followed until the main text-book has been studied. Consequently when it is followed your mind will have been fortified by previous reading and thinking; valuable thoughts of an author will tend to impress you and be remembered, while his trite or erroneous ideas will tend to be ignored.

But after all, what is important is not your attitude or method at the time of reading a book, but the thinking done later. The critical attitude has its shortcomings, for when we are on the lookout for an author's mistakes we often miss the full significance of his truths. On the other hand when "reading for suggestion" we may too often allow an error to pass unquestioned. But both these disadvantages may be overcome if we do enough thinking afterward.

Only one thing I must insist on: make sure you understand every sentence of a book. Do not "guess" you understand it. Do not slide over it in the hope that the author will explain it later. Do not work yourself into the belief that after all it is not really important. Rather than this, better by far do not read the book at all. Not only will you get little or nothing from it but you will be forming the worst of intellectual habits—that of thinking you understand when you do not. If you have made every reasonable effort to understand an author and then have not succeeded, write in the margin "I do not understand this," or draw a line alongside the sentence or passage. If you have to do this too often you should put the volume aside for a time. It is either too advanced for you or it is not worth reading.

As to the thinking you do after reading. Often problems connected with the subject of a book you have read may arise spontaneously in mind, or an objection to a statement may suddenly occur to you when thinking on some other topic. Of course when this happens you should not stifle your thoughts. But besides this, definite periods should be put aside for thinking on what you have read and on the problems you have written. I cannot insist on this too strenuously or too often.

A good task to set before yourself is to take every idea you agree with in a book and try to treat it as a "germ." Tell yourself that you will develop it beyond the point where the author left off. Of course this will not always be possible. You will seldom succeed. But there is nothing like hitching your wagon to a star, and it will do no harm to set this up as an ideal.

A few miscellaneous problems remain to be considered.

How should we deal with authors with whom we disagree fundamentally? Herbert Spencer relates that he twice started Kant's *Critique of Pure Reason*, but disagreeing fundamentally with the first and main proposition he ceased reading. Now to do this is to give an author too much credit for consistency. For even if every other proposition he sets forth is ostensibly a corollary from his leading one, some of them will contain much truth. It is impossible to be consistently wrong. Add to this the possibility that the author may be right on his first proposition after all. However, no book with a viewpoint radically different from our own should be used as a main text, for we would get little benefit from it. If the book is by an obscure author we may safely lay it aside altogether. But if it is by so famous and so bepraised a philosopher as Kant we should at least glance through the entire volume for suggestions.

How many times ought we to read a book? I have already partly answered this in formulating the law of diminishing returns. Few books are worth re-reading. Rather than read one book twice on any given subject it will most often be more profitable to read another book on it. For the second will not only serve as a review of previous knowledge, but will furnish you with new ideas, different aspects and new problems.

Certain books, however, can never be replaced by others. They occupy this position either because they deal with a subject not elsewhere dealt with or because they take an entirely novel aspect, or solely because they are the works of supreme genius, for while the main conclusions reached in works of this last type may be found elsewhere, the *manner of thinking* can never be. These books should be read twice. The main text-book selected on any subject will usually be chosen because it is the best and most comprehensive work on that subject. For this reason it should be read a second time even if such reading is only of the hop, skip and jump variety.

We should not re-read a book immediately upon the first completion but should always allow a long interval to elapse. There are several reasons for this. After an interval we acquire perspective; we are in a position to know

whether a book has done us any good and just
about how much. We may find after this interval that a work of which we thought quite
highly at the time of reading has really not
helped us appreciably either in thought or action. We may find that we have outgrown the
need of it. ·Even if we finally decide to re-read
we shall find the wait of immense help to our
memory. If we re-read a book after an interval
of six months, three years after our second reading we will remember its contents much better
than if we had read it three times in unbroken
succession. Add to this that in the lapse of
time we shall have forgotten most of the work,
and shall therefore approach it the second time
with greater interest than if it were still fresh
in mind; that our experience, reading and thinking in the meantime will make us see every sentence in a different light, enabling us to judge
our own marginal criticisms (if we have made
any) as well as the book, and the advantage of
waiting cannot be doubted. I do not believe it
will ever be necessary to read a book more than
twice, that is, so far as thought and knowledge
are concerned. With books read for their

style or for mere amusement the case is different.

How long should one read at a sitting? Some men find that their thought is choked by reading. Some find it stimulated. But results vary according to the length of time reading is carried on. Reading for very long periods at a stretch often deadens original thought. The writer finds that he nearly always derives benefit from reading for short periods, say ten or fifteen minutes. This is in some measure due to the increased concentration which short periods allow. On the other hand, some people find that a certain momentum is acquired during long reading periods. The reader can only experiment to find how long a period best suits his individual case.

How about concentration? This has been considered in relation to independent thinking, but in reading the problem is somewhat different. In thinking our task is to choose relevant associates. In reading the associates are chosen for us. Our task is to stick to them, instead of following the associates which occur to us either from what we read or from sights and sounds about us. But associates which occur to us from what we read are of two kinds: relevant and irrelevant, and the former should of course be followed out. This however should be done deliberately, in the manner I have previously indicated, and when the vein of suggested thought has been exhausted we should bring attention back to our book. The problem of concentration is not a very serious one in reading. It may sometimes be difficult to concentrate on a book. But it is infinitely easier than concentrating on a problem by unaided independent thought.

The plan of reading I have laid out is merely suggestive. What I chiefly wanted to show was that all books cannot be treated alike, that we cannot lay down dogmatic inflexible rules to apply to every volume. Our method of reading will vary with the nature of a book or of the subject it treats. It will depend upon the books we have already read and even upon the books we contemplate reading later.

The good you get out of reading will depend entirely on how you allow it to affect you. If every book you read suggests more problems, gives you worth-while questions and topics to think about in spare moments, enriches your intellectual life and stimulates your thought, it is performing its proper function. But if you read solely to answer problems you cannot answer for yourself, if every time you are puzzled about anything you run to a book to have it explained, and accept without question the explanation there given; in short, if you use your reading to save yourself from thinking, you had better stop reading altogether. Smoking is a far less harmful form of dissipation.

I have not yet definitely indicated the ratio which time given to reading should bear to time devoted to thinking. I have avoided this because of the many factors to be taken into account. But if the reader happens to have a spare hour to devote to the improvement of his mind, he will not go very far wrong if he gives thirty minutes to reading and thirty minutes to thinking. His thinking may be on the subject he has read, or part of it may be on other problems. That is not so important. But the reader must not imagine that his thinking need be restricted to these thirty minutes or any other thirty minutes. The glorious advantage of thinking is that it can be fitted in at any odd moment. The entire apparatus for carrying it on is always with you. You do not even need a book for it. I remind the reader of this at the risk of repeating myself.

It was pointed out at the beginning of this chapter that the reading of any book is not an end in itself, but should be subordinated to the larger end of obtaining the best from reading in general. But for the sake of clearness our end was temporarily considered as the mastery of some particular subject. I indicated a plan of reading to best serve that end. I also promised that needful qualifications would come later.

In stating the law of diminishing returns it was pointed out that it applied to whole subjects as well as to books, that "past a certain point every book we read on a subject, while it will probably add to our knowledge, will not yield as much return as a book of equal merit on another subject new to us."

While this is true it applies to but a small extent when subjects are read by the method just outlined, for while we do not get as much out of any book as we would out of one of equal merit on another subject, we read it so much faster that the return per time and energy expended is practically as great. This fast reading is made possible by our previous knowledge on the old subject. If the book on the new subject were read in the same manner, we might get little or nothing from it.

With this objection out of the way I suggest that the reader get a specialty. Books read in the ordinary unsystematic fashion, now on this subject and now on that, leave little permanent impression. Even if they do, we feel that though our range of reading may be wide we have at best but a smattering of many things. In the final analysis a smattering of knowledge is in most cases of no more use than total ignorance. Better by far be ignorant of many things and know one thing well, than know many things badly.

Besides the utility of having a specialty is the pleasure we derive. There is always an intense satisfaction in feeling that one is an "expert," an "authority" in some subject. When some Congressman makes an inaccurate remark which trespasses on your specialty you can write a letter to the *Times* or the *Sun* explaining the error of his ways, and incidentally exhibiting your own limitless erudition. When your friends get into an argument on some question within your chosen field they will remark, "Ask John Jones. He ought to know." And even when you have to confess abysmal ignorance on some question outside of your domains, you may still have the satisfaction of believing that people are excusing you within themselves with an "Oh, well, but he knows a lot about someology."

One writer estimates that "fifteen minutes a day or a half hour three days a week devoted to one definite study will make one a master in that field in a dozen years." [6] This statement should interest those people who "haven't the time" to take up any specialty outside their own business, but who spend at least half an hour every day in newspaper or magazine reading—

[6] Edward Griggs, *The Use of the Margin.*

with nothing to show for it at the end of twenty years.

Just what subject you make your specialty I am not at present concerned. It may be aeronautics, astronomy, banking, Greek history, differential calculus, social psychology, electricity, music, philosophy of law, submarines, soap manufacture, religion, metaphysics, sun-motors, education, literary style or the moon. But whatever it is, it ought to be a subject in which you are interested for its own sake—which most frequently means one which you do not make your vocation. If you get tired of it, drop it and take up something in which you are interested. Your thinking and study should be pursued as a pleasure—not as a duty.

If your subject is a narrow one, if let us say it is merely a branch of what is generally considered a science, you should first get a clear. idea of the broad outlines of the science before taking the specialty up. Should you, for instance, select the tariff, begin your study by using as your main text a book on general economics.

Even if you make your specialty an entire

science you will derive great help by reading in other sciences. In ethics, for instance, a knowledge of psychology, biology and sociology will prove of surprising value. This means that for the sake of knowing the specialty itself, if for nothing else, you should not pursue it exclusively. If ever you find yourself in danger of doing this it would be well to lay down a rule that every third or fourth book you read must be one which does not deal with the subject you have chosen as your own.

VIII

WRITING ONE'S THOUGHTS

Reading maketh a full man, conference a ready man, and writing an exact man.—BACON.

ANY attempt to formulate a science or art of thinking would not be complete without at least some discussion of writing. Indeed writing is so closely bound up with thinking that I have been compelled to refer to it several times in the discussion of thought and reading.

I have already spoken of writing as an aid to concentration. I was wont to depreciate it on account of its slowness. But this is practically its only fault. Thoughts come to us when writing which we get in no other way. One is often surprised, when reading something one has written at a previous time, at some of the remarks made. We seem to have temporarily grown wiser than ourselves.

But the great advantage of writing is that it

preserves thought.   What printing has done for humanity in preserving the knowledge of the ages, writing will do for the individual in preserving his own reflections.

When some thought has occurred to us we believe at the time we are thinking it that it is ours forever.   We cannot conceive that it shall ever be forgotten.   Perish that belief!   I have sometimes had an idea occur to me (really!), and have believed it absolutely new, at least so far as I was concerned.   But on looking over things written before, I have found that I had had almost identically the same thought at another time.   Not only did I forget the idea; I did not even recognize it at its second appearance.   To be sure, in these cases the thoughts came a second time.   But thoughts are seldom so obliging.

Therefore when an idea occurs or when you have solved a problem, even a problem suggested by a book, you should immediately put the idea or solution in writing.   You may of course wait until the end of the day.   But the safest way of capturing an idea is to write it the minute after it flashes through your brain, or it may be lost forever. It was with this in mind that in the chapter on reading I advised immediately writing not only ideas but problems which occurred to one. The discovery of a new problem is just as important and necessary for intellectual advance as the solution of an old one. If we do not write our problems we are apt to forget they exist; we put ourselves in danger of assuming without question some proposition which is not true.

To facilitate the writing of your thoughts and meditations I suggest a notebook kept specially for that purpose. In addition to this you should always carry about with you some blank paper and a pencil, so as to be ever ready to jot down anything. To write an idea does not of course imply that you cannot later reject it, or change it, or develop it further.

The elusiveness of thoughts is most strikingly brought out when writing them down. When we are writing a long sentence we have in mind the exact words with which we are going to finish it. But our attention is called for the moment to the physical act of writing, and presto!—the words are gone; we are compelled to end our sentence in a different way. I have mentioned the advantages of shorthand and typewriting for keeping pace with thought. I need merely repeat my advice to use these acquirements if you have them. Thoughts, I must repeat, are fleeting. No device for trapping them should be despised.

Not least among the advantages of a notebook in which to write thoughts is the permanent historical record it gives. Every thought we write should be dated, day, month and year, like a letter. When we come to read over ideas jotted down from time to time in this manner, we shall see before us an intellectual autobiography. We shall see how our recent thoughts compare with those written sometime ago. We shall see just what our opinions were at certain times, and how they have changed. And we shall see whether our mental progress has been marked, or whether we have been standing still.

It may be considered absurd to suggest that every thought you write in your note-book be put in the best style you can command. We are

wont to differentiate "style" and "matter."
It is doubtful whether this distinction is quite
valid. It is doubtful whether we know just what
we mean when we make it. Indeed Arnold
Bennett goes so far as to say:

"Style cannot be distinguished from matter.
When a writer conceives an idea he conceives
it in the form of words. That form of words
constitutes his style, and it is absolutely gov-
erned by the idea. The idea can only exist in
words, it can only exist in one form of words.
You cannot say exactly the same thing in two
different ways. Slightly alter the expression,
and you slightly alter the idea. Surely it is
obvious that the expression cannot be altered
without altering the thing expressed! The
writer, having conceived and expressed an idea,
may, and probably will, 'polish it up.' But
what does he polish up? To say that he pol-
ishes up his style is merely to say that he pol-
ishes up his idea, that he has discovered faults
and imperfections in his idea, and is perfecting
it. The idea exists in proportion as it is expressed; it exists when it is expressed, and not

before. It expresses itself. A clear idea is expressed clearly and a vague idea vaguely." [1]

Mr. Bennett, I suspect, is a victim of exaggeration. But this much is true: Thought and style are mutually dependent to a far greater degree than is generally supposed. Not only will an improvement in a thought improve its wording; an improvement in wording will improve the thought.

Now as to the application of this. I have referred to the occurrence in reading of "inarticulate" objections. The sole reason these are inarticulate is because the objection is too vague even to find expression. In a case like this we should word our objection the best we can, no matter how ridiculous or indefensible it at first sounds. But we should word it in as many ways as possible; we should say it in all different sorts of ways; we should write it in every different kind of way. Gradually our objection will become definite, clear, forceful. In short, we shall not only have improved our way of stating our thought; we shall have improved the thought itself. To study clearness of statement

[1] *Literary Taste.*

or acquisition of vocabulary is to study means of improving thought. Your notebook should not be used solely for the entry of "thoughts" as such, but any striking way of wording a thought which occurs to you should likewise be immediately written.

But while there is some truth in Arnold Bennett's statement that the wording is the thought, from another point of view its very opposite is true. The wording is *never* the thought. Strictly speaking, "thought" is something which can exist only in the mind. It can never be transferred to paper. What then is it that we write? If words and sentences are not thought, what are they? If they are not thought how is it possible to transfer thought through the medium of writing?

The fact is that words, though they are not thought, are the *associates* of thought. You hear the word "horse." Very likely the visual image of a horse arises in mind. This image, idea, notion, "concept," will depend on your experience of particular horses. It will never be a logical abstract of these. It will never be a horse without color, particular size, sex or

breed, as is sometimes thought. It may however have different elements in it from different
horses you have seen. It may be the image of
just one particular horse you remember. But
no such thing as a general concept exists in the
mind. We have a particular image which stands
for all horses. The name of course is general. It—or its definition—may be called the
logical concept. But the name itself is not used
in thought. It is an arbitrary symbol which
serves merely to arouse a particular image associated with it, and this image is dealt with as if
general. This image we shall call the concept.
It is the working concept: the psychological as
opposed to the logical concept.

As your concept of a horse will depend on
your experience of particular horses, another
person's concept will depend on *his* experience
of that animal. And as his éxperience can
never be exactly the same as yours, his concept,
though it may be similar to yours, will not be
the same. Not only will no one else have the
same mental image or concept as you *but you
yourself will never have exactly the same image
twice.* This image will vary with the setting in

which it occurs—with the associates which happen to arouse it. If you are reading about a great battle and the word "horse" is mentioned, a certain kind of horse will suggest itself to you. If you are reading about a grocery wagon and see the word "horse" another kind will suggest itself. This whether the animal is described by adjectives or not. At one time you may think of the horse as in motion, at another time as at rest.

Unfortunately many so-called psychologists seem to consider the concept, even this image-concept, as something fixed in the individual, or at best as only changing with actual experience of the thing conceived. The truth is that the image or images aroused on hearing any word are not the same for two seconds at a time. They are fluid, dynamic; never static, immobile. They are associates of the words in a constant state of flux.[2] When the concept of one individual varies from one moment to the next, how

[2] The most advanced and severe psychologists may object to some statements in this exposition. I admit that a word may be used as the concept, *but only provided it is accompanied by a "fringe" of potential associates.* I also admit that in order to be dealt with as if general, the visual image

must the concepts of different individuals differ from each other!

I have instanced the idea of a horse because it is so simple and concrete. In actual thinking we never meet with a simple separated concept or with a single word; we deal with at least an entire sentence. This means that our images vary even more widely at different times than was the case in the example. It means that the images of other people are at a correspondingly greater variance from ours.

As to the application of all this to writing. We have an idea; thinking it important we decide to jot it down. Now we cannot jot down the idea, but only words associated with it. We cannot even write all the words associated with it, for there are too many. So we write a comparative few; and we say we have written the idea. *But all we have really written is something associated with the idea.* When we read this over at a later time we shall not have the same ideas aroused as were in mind origi-

must be accompanied by such a "fringe." But I do insist that this fringe itself is in a constant state of flux. That is the important point for our present purposes.

nally, but at best only similar ideas. For the associates of words, like all associates, are constantly changing; and thanks to the frailties of human memory exactly the same associates are never aroused twice. So after a long interval they will be much different than at the time we wrote. The reader will often have the experience of "writing a thought" and thinking it very important, but on reading it at another time he will fail to see why he ever considered it worth putting on paper. The truth is that at the time he wrote the idea it probably *was* important, because he had the right concepts. But when he came back to the words he had written they failed to re-suggest the former concepts and associates.

This difference between words and thought is even more strikingly brought out when the written thought is read by some other person than the writer. The writer is likely at least to have approximately the same concepts as at the time of writing. And he is greatly aided by his memory in recalling the concepts and associated ideas previously in mind, the words suggesting these. But when a person reads what some one else has written, he translates the words into the concepts previously connected with them in his own mind. Thus an author can never literally transfer an idea. He can merely put down certain arbitrary symbols, which will serve to arouse a similar thought in his readers. How greatly the reader's thought differs from the author's it is difficult if not impossible to determine, for minds can only communicate by words. It is this difference in associated concept which often makes a reader fail to appreciate the profoundest thoughts of an author, and even, on the other hand, occasionally to see depth where it does not exist.

We come now to the solution of the problem to which this rather extended discussion has been preparatory. How is an author to convey, as nearly as possible, his actual idea? And the answer is: *he should word it in as many different ways as possible.*

If a person had never been to a city and you wanted to give him an idea of it, you would show him photographs taken from different viewpoints. One photograph would correct and supplement the other. And the more photographic viewpoints he saw the more complete and accurate would be his idea—the more his concept would approximate the actual city. But he could never more than approximate; he could never obtain the idea of a man who had visited that city.

An author's language is a photograph of his thought. He can never actually transfer an idea, but by wording it in different ways he can show different photographs of it.

If, for example, a second wording does not conform with the first concept which a reader has formed, the reader will be obliged to modify that concept. And if the idea is repeated in a number of different ways he will have to modify his concept so much that he will gradually more and more approximate the idea of the author.

I remember the story in some educational treatise of an inspector who entered a school room, asked the teacher what she had been giving her class, and finally took up a book and asked the following question, "If you were to dig a hole thousands and thousands of feet deep, would it be cooler near the bottom or near the top, and why?" Not a child answered.

Finally the teacher said, "I'm sure they know the answer but I don't think you put the question in the right way." So taking the book she asked, "In what state is the center of the earth?" Immediately came the reply from the whole class in chorus, "The center of the earth is in a state of *igneous fusion.*" . . .

There is, and has been for the past generation, a great cry in educational circles that we should teach things, not words. In some instances this is inadvisable, even impracticable. But if the teacher in the foregoing story had taken the trouble to word her idea in at least more than one way, she might have implanted a real idea in her pupils. She would at least have found that as it was they had none.

One more question remains. If you are writing a composition, a letter, an essay, or even a book, what is the best way to get down all your thoughts, without losing any of value; to get them down in the best order and in the best style? In other words what is the path of greatest efficiency in transferring thoughts from your mind to paper?

We have already considered such devices as shorthand. Of course dictation, where it is possible, is an obvious advantage. But I mean here to consider the aspects of the problem which apply more especially to compositions of some length.

It is related of Auguste Comte that he composed his books by thinking them over down to the minutest details, down to the very phraseology of the sentences, before penning a single word, but that when he came to writing he could turn out an astounding amount of work in a given time. Unless a person have a remarkable memory, however, he will forget most of what he has thought by the time he comes to writing it. Comte's method might nevertheless be profitably applied to short sections of compositions. And where conciseness or perspicuity are desired, it will often be found useful to think out an entire sentence before writing a word of it.

Perhaps the best way of ensuring efficiency in writing is by the card system. This consists in writing on a separate card every valuable idea that occurs to you, immediately after it occurs.

When you finally come to writing you can arrange these cards in any order desired, throwing out the ideas you no longer consider important, and adding those which are necessary to complete or round out the work.

IX

THINGS WORTH THINKING ABOUT

*The man who cannot wonder, who does not habit-
ually wonder, is but a pair of spectacles behind which
there is no eye.*—CARLYLE.

U P to now I have treated exclusively of *how*
to think, but have made no mention of
what to think. I have treated of the best methods of dealing with different subjects and questions; I have not considered what subjects or
problems are most worth dealing with.

Of course the important thing is that you
do think. It is not absolutely essential that the
results of your thinking are results which can
be directly made use of. Thinking is an end
in itself. Most men imagine that "thinking for
the sake of thinking" may appeal to philosophers, but means nothing to them, as they like
to think only when by so doing they can forward some practical end. These people do
themselves an injustice.

Perhaps you, O reader, are among them. If so, let me appeal to your personal experience. Have you ever tried to solve a toy puzzle, tried to take the two wire hooks apart without bending them? Or have you ever stopped to tackle a problem on the family page of your evening or Sunday newspaper? "A grocer buys fifteen dozen eggs, he sells—" you know what I mean. You admit that you have. Exactly. You have been thinking for the mere sake of thinking.

If you protest that you didn't care about the thinking, that you took no pleasure in the thinking, which was merely incidental, but that what really urged you on and gave you pleasure was the solution of the puzzle, you are again deceiving yourself. The thinking was not incidental. Thinking and problem solving are identical. The fact is that you set yourself to solving a problem, to removing a mental hindrance, for the mere sake of getting the answer, with absolutely no thought of what you were going to do with the answer when you got it.

But if you can derive so much pleasure from thinking which you cannot put to use, how much greater should be your pleasure when your con-

clusions can be utilized? For when you think
of something useful, you have not only the present pleasure of solving your problem, but the
ulterior pleasure of applying your solution to
action, or to the solution of some further problem. And while I again admit that thinking is
an end in itself, this does not prevent it from
being at the same time a means to some further
end. After all is said there is really no reason
why we should be prejudiced against problems
or subjects that are useful.

The mere decision that we should think of
useful questions is insufficient. Very few questions are without *some* use. Even the solution
of the family page puzzle might some day be
useful in solving a similar problem arising in
your own business; and even if this never came
to pass you might spring the puzzle on your
friends, and make yourself socially more interesting. Thought given to a question in a debating book now before me, "Resolved, that
Ferocious Wild Beasts are more to be dreaded
than Venomous Reptiles," might result in
knowledge which would come handy in selecting equipment if one decided to journey to the

wilderness of South America. But there are
millions of problems of as much use as these;
and it is not within the power of one lone mor-
tal, of years three score and ten, to compass
even a corner of them. Our question is not—
what problems are of use?, but—of *how much*
use are certain problems?, or stated in another
way,—what is the *relative* utility of problems?

Any adequate consideration of this question
would involve the selection of some criterion for
utility, and the testing of individual problems
by that criterion. But to treat such a question
with anything like justice is beyond the scope of
this book; it would require almost a volume in
itself. It is almost the same as the problem,
What knowledge is of most worth?, and the most
masterly treatise on that question which has
ever been written can be found in Herbert Spencer's epoch-making little work, *Education*. I
sincerely hope that the reader study this. But
I hope éven more earnestly that before he does
so he first think the problem out independently,
for it is one of the most important he can put
before himself.

But our present question—that of the relative

importance of problems—is slightly different
from that of the relative importance of knowledge. The first deals with thought and the
second with information, or the materials of
thought; the first with a process of getting
knowledge and the second with knowledge itself.

I believe for example that a knowledge of his
own body and of the laws of health is the most
·valuable a man can have, but there are few
problems concerning the body which I would include in the first rank. There are several reasons for this. In the first place, while it may
be true that such questions *taken as a whole*
are more important than any other class of
questions, taken separately they are relatively
minor; there are no one or two questions of all-
encompassing importance to which all the others
are subsidiary. Moreover, such questions,
while they undoubtedly require thought for their
solution, depend to a relatively great extent on
observation and experiment. No sane medical
student would sit down and follow out a lengthy
course of reasoning as to where the heart is;
he would merely observe or dissect, or consult
the book of a man who had dissected, and save

mental fatigue. Not least of all, questions of physiology require extensive, highly technical and detailed information—information which requires years of special study to acquire—before any thinking that is at all safe can be put upon them. So in estimating the relative value of problems, there are other considerations besides the value of knowledge.

But it is not my purpose here to discuss the general principles upon which the selection of worth-while questions should be made. That task I leave to the reader. I have chosen rather the concrete path of suggesting a list of questions which I consider of great import. I believe that no matter how much thought the reader gives to any one of them he will not be losing his time.

I have elsewhere pointed out that the more knowledge a man has the more problems he will have. It is equally true that unless a man has some knowledge on a subject he will not be able to appreciate or even understand some of its most important problems. It is only when we begin to think of subjects that we discover problems and realize their significance. In stating

most of the following problems, therefore, I
have often thought it necessary to add a few
sentences in explanation, and have sometimes
stated a question in a variety of forms in order
to more clearly convey the thought.

*Are specific characteristics, acquired during
the lifetime of an individual, inherited by his
offspring?* I have referred so often to this
problem and its importance that further explanation is hardly necessary. "Characteristics" of course refer to intellectual and moral
as well as physical characteristics.

*What is the influence of the individual mind
on society and of social environment on the individual?*

*Does the form of government determine the
character of a people, or does the character of a
people determine their form of government?*
Or do government and character react on each
other, and how? The same question may be
asked of all other social institutions. Does
the religion of a people determine their character, or does the character of a people determine
their religion? This whole problem is some-

what similar to that immediately preceding, regarding the interaction of the individual and the social mind.

Is society for the benefit of the individual or is the individual for the benefit of society?

Should the jurisdiction of the government be extended or curtailed? Or should it be extended in some directions and curtailed in others? Does the answer to this problem depend on the answer to the previous one? Another form of the same problem is: What is the proper sphere of government?

Should the government grant monopolies? Patents, for example?

What would be the most practicable plan for abolishing or minimizing war? Those who do not wish to beg the previous question may first ask whether it is always desirable to prevent war, whether war is always an evil. What is the effect of war on the physical future of the race? on national and individual character? on government? on national liberty? on personal liberty? What are the ethics of war? for aggression? for territorial conquest? for "national honor"? for defense of a weaker nation? for defense against invasion? What is the effect of preparedness? of universal preparedness? of preparedness of an individual nation? In each case what are the principles on which the extent of preparedness should be determined? What are the fundamental causes of war? How can they be removed? Is it possible to remove all of them?

Which is the rightful owner of land, the community or the individual? To state the problem in another form: Should private land ownership be abolished?

Who should be entitled to vote? This of course is a question similar to woman suffrage, but it is much broader. It deals not only with the qualification of sex, but of age. Should any one under twenty-one have the vote? The validity of property and educational qualifications should also be considered.

How should the relations of the sexes be regulated? Put in slightly narrower and perhaps less objectionable form: What would be just laws governing marriage and divorce?

What is the effect of attempted State interference with the law of supply and demand?

Does the unrestricted working out of this law forward ultimate justice? Just what is the validity and the meaning of the expression "The *law* of supply and demand"? The question could be taken up in connection with minimum wage laws, railroad rate regulations, "extra crew" laws, etc.

Which is the best policy: free trade, revenue tariff, or protective tariff? Or under what conditions is each best? With what classes of commodities?

What would be an equitable and sound currency system? This question is somewhat technical, and would have to be considered in the form of a number of subsidiary problems. Ought money to have an intrinsic value? What is the effect of "fiat" paper currency on money of intrinsic value and on prices? The effect of credit? The effect of fluctuations in the supply of gold? Ought there be a double standard or a multiple standard? etc.

Should conduct be judged by the pleasure or happiness it yields? Stated in another form, almost a different problem: Is utility a good moral guide?

Should conduct be judged by its tendency to produce individual well-being, or should it be judged by its tendency to produce the well-being of all humanity, or of all sentient beings? This problem cannot be lightly dismissed in favor of universal well-being. This becomes apparent when we attempt to give an undogmatic and non-question-begging answer to the query: Why should a man act for the benefit of others?

No science is more provocative of thought than ethics. The question of whether acts should be declared good or bad as they tend to produce pleasure or happiness, either individual or in humanity as a whole, or whether "virtue" or "morality" is an end in itself, is one of the most subtle and elusive we can attempt to solve; no matter which answer we give we are brought into logical and psychological dilemmas from which it seems impossible to escape. This is also true of the problem of whether our knowledge of what constitutes right and wrong comes from experience or from intuition.

The broadest form of the ethical problem,

which includes the two preceding italicized problems, is:

What is the proper criterion for determining right and wrong conduct? Or even less dogmatic: Can there be a criterion for determining right and wrong conduct, and what is it?

Somewhat allied with the ethical problem is that problem of problems: how to live? By this is meant how to put the most into life and get the most out of it; what vocation to follow; what hobbies, amusements, avocations to take up; how to plan time by months, by weeks, by days, by hours. How much time and energy do certain activities deserve? How much can we afford to give them? Restated: what activities are of most worth?

Of course every one does think of problems connected with the art of living. But he thinks of them as little unconnected questions. Rarely indeed does any one go about the solution of the general problem of living in an orderly, systematic manner. To insist upon the broad practical bearings of the problem would be unnecessary, absurd. By its very nature it is the most "practical" question we can ask. Any particular solution or treatment may be impractical, but this does not affect the question itself.

What are the respective influences of environment (education, experience, etc.) and innate tendencies in determining character? Which is the greater determinant?

Does pleasure depend upon the satisfaction of instinctive desires, or do desires for certain activities depend upon the pleasure accompanying the previous performance of such activities? Does an activity or the possession of an object give us pleasure because we have previously desired it, or do we desire an activity or an object because we have previously obtained pleasure from it? Or do pleasure and desire interact, and just how? The solution of this psychological problem is of tremendous importance in ethics.

Does the mind depend entirely on the brain? That is, are all thoughts, emotions, feelings, due to material changes in the brain? The answer we give to this problem may determine our answer to the question of immortality.

What knowledge is of most worth? I have so fully discussed the importance of this question and the method of proceeding with its solution that further explanation is needless.

One sphere of thought where the thinker is compelled to be original; where it is practically impossible for him to fall into beaten tracks, is invention. But there is useless as well as useful invention. A man's ambition may range all the way from inventing a machine to harness directly the limitless power of the sun, down to devising a tenacious tip for shoelaces. But he should be careful about inventing something already patented. He should be even more careful to avoid inventing something for which there is no demand. One of Edison's first patents was for a machine to register quickly the votes of legislative assemblies. And it worked. But the legislative assemblies didn't want it, because they didn't want their votes quickly registered. That would have ended good old filibuster methods. Another invention of great uselessness which has been several times attempted is a machine to write words just like the human hand writes them. There are really so many useful things which do not exist and for which there is a demand, that it seems quite a pity nine out of ten patents in the files at Washington are for things inutile. If the would-be inventor cannot himself think of something really needed, almost any big patent attorney house will send him an entire book of suggestions on "What to Invent."

Invention usually requires highly technical knowledge, not to speak of facilities for experiment and a well-supplied purse. But nothing gives more solid satisfaction to its creator than a successful appliance. While the conscientious philosopher is constantly harassed by doubts as to whether, after all, he has discovered truth; the inventor need not worry. His machine either works or it does not work, and he *knows* the truth of his thought thereby. On the other hand the philosopher will always have *some* thoughts. Be they true or not they may at least be interesting and worth recording, whereas the inventor may toil on for years and years with absolutely nothing to show for his exertion at the end. . . .

There are a number of problems that are not of great "practical" importance, but whose theoretic value is so transcendent as to compel attention. Among these are certain problems in psychology, but more especially in metaphysics, philosophy and even religion, insofar as religion can be said to have problems.

Is there a God and is it possible for man to learn anything of His nature? Some readers may object to the first part of this question. But I state it because I am anxious to avoid dogmatism.

Is the soul immortal? What do we mean by the soul? Does science disprove the life after death?

What is the test of truth? How shall we know truth when we have it? What after all is "truth"?

Are our wills free, or are our actions predetermined? Some may object to this way of stating the question. Much confusion exists as to the meaning of the problem. A different way of stating it would lead to different treatment. What is the "will"? What do we mean by "free"? What do we mean by "predetermined"?

The problem of existence. How did the universe come into being? This is the last problem in which interest can be stimulated from without. No matter in how many different ways he phrases it, a writer cannot convey this sense of mystery to another. It must arise from within. Most of the time we accept, we take for granted, the universe and the existent order of things, and it requires the greatest effort to keep alive our mystification and doubt for even short periods.

The list of questions foregoing is of course merely suggestive. It is impossible to select, say twenty-five questions, and pronounce them the twenty-five most important that can be asked. I fully realize there are questions of greater importance than some I have propounded. But I have not gone so far as to advise that every one of these should be thought over. The list has been given merely for thought stimulation, and to indicate what is meant by "worth while" questions.

Unfortunately I have not been able to explain why most of these are so important. To have done so would have required too much time for each individual problem. It would have drawn us too far out of our subject. The reader must find out or sense the importance for himself.

Practically all of the problems given in the list come under one of the sciences, especially if we count metaphysics or philosophy as a science, which it is in so far as it is organized knowledge. This may seem somewhat narrow. Now I admit there are important problems which are not included in any science. But there are very few. As soon as deep thought is given to a problem its treatment becomes systematic. It either falls into one of the sciences or a new science evolves about it. John Stuart Mill once started a journal in which he promised himself to put one thought a day, but he did not permit himself to record there any thought on a problem falling within one of the special sciences. None of the thoughts he put in the journal is of any great value. It came to an abrupt end in about two months.

It may be objected that though the questions selected are most important *in themselves*, there are other things more worth thinking about, because of the mental discipline they yield. Now putting aside the fact that questions important

in themselves should be dealt with ultimately—
that mental discipline would be useless unless
applied to important problems—I must voice my
suspicion that the most useful questions are also
the best for training the mind.   It may be true
that punching the bag will help a prizefighter in
boxing.   But other things equal, a man who has
spent one week in actual boxing is better prepared to enter the prize ring than one who has
devoted a month to bag punching.   The best
practice for boxing is boxing.   The best practice for solving important questions is solving
important questions.

Nor do I admit the contention is valid that
one problem rather than another should be
thought of because it is "deeper."   We cannot
truthfully say that psychology is a "deeper"
science than ethics, or that metaphysics is deeper
than psychology, or vice versa.   Most subjects
and most problems are just as deep as we care
to make them.   Their depth depends entirely on
how deep we go into them.   This applies especially to the so-called philosophical sciences.
We may give them shallow treatment or we may
give them profound treatment.   But we shall

usually find that the deepest questions are the
most important questions. For the most important questions have generally attracted the
greatest minds; consequently they have been
given the deepest treatment; and when a man
reads the attempted solutions of these great
minds his thoughts tend toward this deeper
plane. Of course certain problems, especially
in mathematics, can be dealt with by only one
method. In this case we may properly speak
of some problems being objectively deeper or at
least more difficult than others.

Some objections may be offered to several of
the questions in my list, on the ground that they
are invalid. Such problems as the immortality
of the soul and the problem of existence may be
declared inscrutable, unsolvable. Such a problem as "Is society for the benefit of the individual or is the individual for the benefit of society?" may be said to imply that society is
something which has been voluntarily formed
like the State. It may be declared that this is
not the case; it may be objected that this question is meaningless. All these objections may
be justified. But their truth cannot be deter-

mined until we actually attempt a solution. The determination of the validity of a problem is part of the problem.

We come now to the question of what is most worth reading. The simplest answer is that that is most worth reading which is most worth thinking about, and therefore we should read those books which deal with such problems as I have indicated. But this counsel needs to be supplemented.

A conservative estimate places the number of books in the world at 4,500,000. (This estimate was made before the war broke out, and the war-books by now have doubtless brought the number to 5,000,000.) This does not mean books as collections of printed sheets of paper bound together—books as physical objects—for if it did the number would be immensely greater. It means 4,500,000 (or more) separate and distinct treatises. If you were to read one book every two weeks, you would read about twenty-five a year, and if you read for fifty years you would cover 1,250. One book in every three thousand six hundred! (3,600!)

From this it is apparent that even the most omnivorous reader, even the reader who can cover a book swiftly by efficient skipping, will at least have to ask himself before beginning a volume, "Is this a book in a thousand? Can I afford to read this at the cost of missing nine hundred and ninety-nine others?" And most men who ask this question will have to substitute the number five thousand, or even ten thousand.

Nine-tenths of our reading is on mere chance recommendation, passing whim or by sheer accident. We catch sight of a book on a library table. Having nothing better to do we pick it up; we start perusing it. Every book read in this way means a sinful waste of time. To be sure, a book read in this chance manner *might* (accidentally) be very good—even better than some you would have planned for; but this will happen seldom, and is never a justification of the practice. By going a round about way to a place a man might stumble across a lost pocketbook, but this would not justify taking round about ways.

The first thing needed, then, is that we should

plan our reading. Perhaps the best way to do this would be to make out a list of the books we intend to read for the coming year, or say a list of from a dozen to twenty-five volumes, and then read them in the order listed. Another good plan is to jot down the title of every book we intend to read, and keep the list about with us. Then when we meet with a book which we think would be good to read, or which we feel we simply must read, we can before starting it glance at our list. The formidable array we find there will probably induce us either to give up entirely our intention to read the book before us, or at least to put it somewhere on the list which will allow more important books to be read first.

Some people cannot endure planning their reading in this manner. It grates on them to think they are tied down to any sort of program; it seems to deprive them of the advantages of spontaneous interest. Well, if you cannot plan your reading prospectively, at least plan it retrospectively. If you cannot keep a list of books you *intend* to read, at least keep a list of books you *have* read. Refer to this from time to time. See whether you have been reading uniformly good literature. See whether you have been reading too much on one topic and not enough on another, and what topics you have been long neglecting. But at best this method is a poor substitute for planning your reading prospectively.

We should plan not only with regard to topics and subjects, but with regard to authors. Obviously if two men of equal ability both study the same subject, one will get more out of his study than the other if he reads authors who treat the subject on a deeper plane—provided of course he understands them.

Whether consciously or not, we tend to imitate the authors we read. If we read shallow books we are forced, while reading them, to do shallow thinking. Our plane of thought tends toward the plane of thought of the authors we study; we acquire either habits of careful critical thinking, or of dogmatic lack of thinking.

This emphasizes the importance of reading the best books, and *only* the best books. Our plane of thinking is determined not alone by the good books we read, but by all the books we read; it tends toward the *average*. Most men imagine that when they read a good book they get a certain amount of good out of it, and that this good will stay with them undiminished. Provided they read a certain number of serious books, they see no reason why they should not read any number of superficial or useless books, or any amount of ephemeral magazine or newspaper literature. They expect the serious reading to benefit them. They do not expect the shallow reading to harm them. This is just as if they were to buy and eat unnutritious and indigestible food, and excuse themselves on the ground that they ate nourishing and digestible food along with it.

The analogy may be carried further. As it is the average of the physical food you digest which ultimately determines the constitution of your body, so it is the average of the mental food you absorb which determines the constitution of your mind. One good meal will not offset a week of bad ones; one good book will never offset any number of poor books. Further, as no one has a perfect memory, you do not retain all you read any more than you retain all you

eat. Therefore if you do not want your mind
to retrogress, you should not rest satisfied with
books already read, but should continue to read
books at least as good as any previous. As at
any given time your bodily health—so far as it
depends on food—is mainly determined by the
meals of the last few days or weeks, so is your
mental health dependent on the last few books
you have read.

One of the first things we should look to in
selecting books is their comprehensiveness.
To quote Arnold Bennett: "Unless and until
a man has formed a scheme of knowledge, be it
but a mere skeleton, his reading must necessarily be unphilosophical. He must have attained to some notion of the interrelations of the
various branches of knowledge before he can
properly comprehend the branch of knowledge
in which he specializes." [1]   As an aid in forming this scheme of knowledge, Mr. Bennett suggests Herbert Spencer's *First Principles*. I
heartily endorse his choice. I would add to it
the essay on *The Classification of the Sciences*
by the same author.

[1] *Literary Taste.*

These works are classics, and one of the most regrettable of difficulties is that of getting people to read the classics. Mention to a man Darwin's *Origin of Species* or *Descent of Man,* and he will reply, "Oh, yes, that's the theory that says men descended from monkeys." Satisfied that he knows all there is to know about it, he never reads any of Darwin's works. Now passing over the fact that the theory does not assert that man descended from monkeys and never intended to assert it;—what a compliment to Darwin's thought and brevity to assume that all his books can be summed up in a phrase! But Darwin is not the only sufferer. If we come across the title of a classic often enough, and hear a lot of talk "about it and about" and a few quotations from it, we gradually come to believe we know all the contents worth knowing. This is why Shakespeare, and in fact most of the classics, are so seldom actually read, and why we go for our serious reading to a book on "How to Read Character from Handwriting" or to a sensational volume on prostitution by one of our modern "sociologists." The only way we can keep ourselves from such stuff is to lay out some definite end, some big objective, to be attained; and before reading a book we should ask how that helps us to attain it.

I have not given a formal list of books worth reading, nor do I intend to; one of the reasons being that the work has been done so well by others. Ever since Sir John Lubbock published his list of one hundred best books, the number of selections has been legion. Charles Eliot's selection for his *Five Foot Shelf* is to be commended, and a little volume by Frank Parsons *The World's Best Books*. Of course our purpose is special:—to find the best books for making thinkers; but the remarks already made should aid the reader sufficiently in making his own selection from these lists. As previously pointed out, if the reader is studying a specialty he can usually find a fairly well selected bibliography at the end of the article on that specialty in any standard encyclopedia.

The reader probably sees clearly by now that it is impossible to do his own thinking in every case; that if he is to have sound knowledge on important questions he must have the courage to be ignorant of many things. How much trouble to go to in any particular case it is difficult to say.

We can lay it down as a general principle that questions of the highest importance, such as those of which I have given a suggestive list— questions which deal with facts known or easily ascertainable, and which depend for their right solution more on thinking than on anything else—a man should solve for himself, and should take the greatest caution in so doing. On the other hand, questions of the highest importance which depend for their solution mainly on full and detailed knowledge of highly technical facts which lie outside of one's specialty, should be dealt with by consulting authorities and taking their word for it.

There still remains the great mass of questions which are relatively unimportant, but continually coming up in our daily life, the answers to which greatly influence our conduct. Time forbids us not only from thinking these out for ourselves, but even from consulting an authority—for the selection of an authority often involves almost as much intellectual responsibility as self-thinking. The only thing we can do is to accept the verdict of popular opinion.

Custom, convention and popular belief, no matter how many times they have been overthrown, have fairly reliable foundations. Popular ideas, to be sure, are products of mere unorganized experience. They are empirical; seldom if ever scientific. But though they are founded on experience which is *unorganized,* they are founded on so much of it that they are worthy of respect. Society could not long exist if it persisted in acting on beliefs altogether wrong, though it is safe to say that popular ideas are never more than approximately right. But unless and until you have either thoroughly thought over a question for yourself or have consulted an acknowledged and trustworthy authority, it is best tentatively to accept and act on common belief. To think and act differently, merely for the sake of being different, is unprofitable and dangerous, all questions of ethics aside.

X

THINKING AS AN ART

I discovered, though unconsciously and insensibly, that the pleasure of observing and reasoning was a much higher one than that of skill and sport.—DARWIN's *Autobiography*.

TO know is one thing; to do another. To know the science of thinking is not to possess the art of thinking. Yet I doubt not that there are readers who having finished, would deem it sufficient that they had the knowledge, and would feel they had gotten all the good or harm out of this book that there is in it. They would put it aside. They would think no more of it.

The trouble with these good people (unfortunately I speak of the overwhelming majority) is that they expect information to apply itself. They expect that once they have learnt a thing they will act according to their knowledge.

This is the very last thing a normal human being does.

The only way we can ever get ourselves to apply knowledge is to do so by what will at first be a conscious effort. We shall have to devote much attention to it. Old established custom will have to be broken. We do not act according to knowledge; we act according to habit. Even after we have decided, for instance, that we ought to give a little independent thinking to a subject before reading about it, we shall very likely continue to read books without previous thought.

Some people may imagine that the reason we do not practice what we learn is that we do not remember what we learn. They are mistaken. When learning German, I had much difficulty in knowing what prepositions required the genitive, dative or accusative cases. I finally learnt all of them alphabetically in their respective groups, and could rattle them off at a rate which would make most native Germans blush for envy. The only trouble was that when I came to an actual sentence requiring one of these prepositions I continually forgot to apply my knowledge. Some one would have to point an error out to me before it would occur to me to do so. Even then I would have to think long before the proper case occurred.

But while it is not true that we fail to practice a thing merely because we fail to remember it, it is true that if we do not practice we are not very likely to remember it. The only way we could remember would be by constant rereading, for knowledge unused tends to drop out of mind. Knowledge used does not need to be remembered; practice forms habits and habits make memory unnecessary. The rule is nothing; the application is everything.

Practice being the thing needful, it is essential that we put aside a certain amount of time for it. Unless you lay out a definite program, unless you put aside, say, one-half hour every day, for pure downright independent thinking, you will probably neglect to practice at all. One-half hour out of every twenty-four seems little enough. You may think you can fit it in with no trouble. But no matter how shamelessly you have been putting in your time, you have been doing *something* with it. In order to get in

your thirty minutes of thinking, you will have
to put aside something which has been habitually
taking up a half hour of your day.   You cannot
expect simply to add thinking to your other activities.   Some other activity must be cut down
or cut out.[1]

You may think me quite lenient in advising
only one-half hour a day.   You may even go so
far as to say that one-half hour a day is not
enough.   Perhaps it isn't.   But I am particularly anxious to have some of the advice in this
book followed.   And I greatly fear that if I advised more than a half hour most readers would
serenely neglect my advice altogether.   After
you have been able for a month to devote at least
one-half hour a day to thinking, you may then,
if you choose, extend the time.   But if you attempt to do too much at once, you may find it so
inconvenient, if not impracticable, that you may
give up attempting altogether.   Throughout
the book I have constantly kept in mind that I
wish my advice followed.   I have therefore laid
down rules which may reasonably be adhered to

[1] And consult Arnold Bennett's *How to Live on 24 Hours
a Day*.

by an average human, rules which do not require a hardened asceticism to apply, and rules which have occasionally been followed by the author himself. In this last respect, I flatter myself, the present differs from most books of advice.

Above all I urge the reader to avoid falling into that habit so prevalent and at the same time so detrimental to character:—acquiescing in advice and not following it. You should view critically every sentence in this book. Wherever you find any advice which you think needless, or which requires unnecessary sacrifice to put into practice, or is wrong, you should so mark it. And you should think out for yourself what would be the best practice to follow. But when you agree with any advice you see here, you should make it your business to follow it. The fact that part of the advice may be wrong is no reason why you should not follow the part that is right.

Most people honestly intend to follow advice, and actually start to do it, but . . . They try to practice everything at once. As a result they end by practicing nothing. The secret of practice is to learn thoroughly one thing at a time.

As already stated, we act according to habit. The only way to break an old habit or to form a new one is to give our whole attention to the process. The new action will soon require less and less attention, until finally we shall do it automatically, without thought—in short, we shall have formed another habit. This accomplished we can turn to still others.

As an example let us take the different methods of looking at questions considered in the second chapter. Most readers will glance over these methods, and agree that they are very helpful—and the next problem which perplexes them will probably be solved by no method at all, or will be looked at from one standpoint only.

About the best, perhaps the only way by which the reader could get himself to use habitually every valuable method possible, would be to take one of the methods, say the evolutionary, and consciously apply it, or attempt to apply it, to a whole list of problems. In this way he could learn the possibilities and limits of that particular method. Again, he could take an individual problem and consciously attempt to apply every possible method to its solution. He could continue such practice until he had so formed the habit of using method that it would be employed almost unconsciously. Concentration, method in book reading, and all the other practices here advocated should be learned in the same conscious, painstaking way, one thing at a time, until thoroughly ingrained. It must be left to the reader's own ingenuity to devise the best methods of acquiring each particular habit.

Of course it is possible to do a thing well— it is possible to follow the rule for doing it— without knowing the rule. If a man take a live interest in a subject he will naturally tend to look at it from a number of different viewpoints. If he be eternally on the lookout for errors and fallacies in his own thinking he will gradually evolve a logic of his own. And this logic will be concrete, not abstract; it will be something built into, an integral part of, concrete thought, and he will be constantly strengthening the habit of using it. Compared with the logic of the books it may be crude, but it will not consist of mere rules, which can be recited but which are seldom applied.

So with grammar. Instance the writer's experience with German. Few native Germans could recite offhand what prepositions govern the genitive, dative and accusative, even if they knew what was meant by these terms. But they would (most of them) use these cases correctly, and without the least thought. The educated Englishman or American flatters himself that his correct speech is due to his study of grammar. This is far from true. His speech is due to unconscious imitation of the language of the people with whom he comes into contact, and of the books he reads. And needless to say, the cultivated man comes into contact with other cultivated men and with good literature; the ignoramus does not.

Most of our thinking is influenced in this way. The great thinkers of the past improved their innate powers not by the study of rules for thinking, but by reading the works of other great thinkers, and unconsciously imitating their habitual method and caution.

The fact to remember is that a rule is something that has been formulated after the thing which it rules. It is merely an abstract of cur-

rent practice or of good practice. Rules are
needful because they teach in little time what
would otherwise require much experience to
learn, or which we might never discover for ourselves at all. They help us to learn things right
in the beginning; they prevent us from falling
into wrong habits. The trouble with unsupple-
mented imitation, conscious or unconscious, is
that we tend to imitate another's faults along
with his virtues. Rules enable us to distinguish,
especially if we have learned the reason for the
rules.

But practice and rules should not be compared
as if they were opposed. The true road is
plenty of practice with conscientious regard to
rule. It may be insisted that this has its limits;
that there is a point beyond which a man cannot
improve himself. I admit that practice has its
limits. It may be true that there is a point beyond which a man cannot advance. But nobody knows those limits and no one can say
when that point has come.

No two individuals profit in the same degree
by the same practice. With a given amount one
man will always improve faster than another.

But the slower man may keep up with his more speedy brother by more practice. I shall not repeat here the fable of the hare and the tortoise. But any one who has discovered a flaw in his mental make-up, any one who believes that he cannot concentrate, or that his memory is poor, and that therefore he can never become a thinker, should find consolation in the words of William James:

"Depend upon it, no one need be too much cast down by the discovery of his deficiency in any elementary faculty of the mind. . . . The total mental efficiency of a man is the resultant of all his faculties. He is too complex a being for any one of them to have the casting vote. If any one of them do have the casting vote, it is more likely to be the strength of his desire and passion, the strength of the interest he takes in what is proposed. Concentration, memory, reasoning power, inventiveness, excellence of the senses—all are subsidiary to this. No matter how scatter-brained the type of a man's successive fields of consciousness may be, if he really *care* for a subject, he will return to it incessantly from his incessant wanderings, and first

and last do more with it, and get more results
from it, than another person whose attention
may be more continuous during a given interval,
but whose passion for the subject is of a more
languid and less permanent sort.'' [2]

[2] *Talks to Teachers.*

XI

BOOKS ON THINKING

THE reader who desires to study further on the subject of thinking will find a wide field before him—but he will have to search in cosmopolitan quarters. While much has been written on thinking, it has been in an incidental manner, and has found its way into books written mainly to illuminate other subjects. Among the few books or essays devoted exclusively or mainly to thinking may be mentioned:—John Locke, *The Conduct of the Understanding;* Isaac Watts, *The Improvement of the Mind;* Arnold Bennett, *Mental Efficiency;* T. Sharper Knowlson, *The Art of Thinking;* Arthur Schopenhauer, *On Thinking for Oneself,* in his *Essays.* The last is especially recommended. It is only about a dozen pages long, and is the most stimulating essay written on the subject. This, together with John Locke's *Conduct* (which, by the way, is also fairly short) may be considered the two "classics" in the meager literature on thinking.

There is an extensive literature on the psychology of reasoning, on the "positive" science of thinking. The best single work on this subject is John Dewey's *How We Think.* William James' chapter on *Reasoning* in his *Principles of Psychology* might also be consulted with profit. S. S. Colvin's, *The Learning Process* contains some interesting chapters bearing on thought.

On method, the amount of literature is even more imposing than that on the psychology of reasoning. Probably the most thorough book is Stanley Jevon's *The Principles of Science,* though this, consisting of two volumes, will require quite some ambition to attack. A good recent short work is J. A. Thomson, *Introduction to Science.* Herbert Spencer's short essay, *An Element in Method,* in his *Various Fragments* might also be mentioned. Of those works treating method mainly from a corrective standpoint, I have already mentioned Jevon's *Elementary Lessons in Logic. The* authoritative and most comprehensive book on logic is still

John Stuart Mill's great tome. Of course this list of books on method, as well as that on the psychology of reasoning, cannot pretend to be more than merely suggestive. If the reader desires an extensive bibliography in either of these subjects he will probably find it in one of the books mentioned.

On doubt and belief, William Clifford, *The Ethics of Belief*, and William James, *The Will to Believe*, might be read. The viewpoints of the two essays are in almost direct contradiction.

On reading, Alexander Bain's *The Art of Study*, in his *Practical Essays*, will be found useful. Bacon's essay *On Studies*, which is not more than a couple pages long, contains more concentrated wisdom on the subject than is to be found anywhere.

On subjects most worth thinking about, the reader cannot do better than read Herbert Spencer's essay *What Knowledge is of Most Worth?* in his *Education*. As to books most worth reading, consult the lists of John Morley, Sir John Lubbock, and Frederic Harrison; Sonnenschein's *Best Books* (in two volumes); Baldwin's *The Book Lover;* Dr. Eliot's *Five Foot Shelf* and Frank Parson's *The World's Best Books,* previously referred to.

On the art of living—the art of planning time so as to have room for thinking, as well as valuable hints as to how that thinking is to be carried out—consult Arnold Bennett, *How to Live on Twenty-four Hours a Day,* and E. H. Griggs, *The Use of the Margin* (both very, very small books).

Finally, there is much useful material, as well as incalculable inspiration, to be obtained from the intellectual and literary biographies of great thinkers. Especially is this true of autobiography. Among others may be mentioned the autobiographies of John Stuart Mill and Herbert Spencer, and an autobiographical fragment by Charles Darwin.

THE END

Printed in the USA
CPSIA information can be obtained
at www.ICGtesting.com
LVHW010232300923
759721LV00005B/394

9 781019 369227